How to be a
sex
goddess

How to be a
sex
goddess

Sarah Tomczak

BARNES
& NOBLE
BOOKS
NEW YORK

Contents

There's something about her...

She's as hot as hell, and she knows it. She's the kind of girl who sashays down the street like she owns it, walking tall in her killer heels and classy threads. She loves her body, and she charms the socks off everyone she meets – guys will do literally anything to get with her. She's a minx between the sheets. She's a sex goddess... and she could be you.

Sounds unlikely? You can drop that attitude for a start. You're about to take a journey from girl to goddess and this book is your guide. No matter how un-goddess-like you're feeling right this second, between these covers you'll find everything you need to turn yourself into a white hot, *femme fatale*. You'll develop kick-ass confidence, learn to celebrate your shape, cultivate amazing style, and work it all to get everything and *anyone* you want. Of course being a *sex* goddess means having spine-tingling experiences in the sack too, and by the time you're done reading this, you'll have him begging for more.

How do I know all this? Easy. I am a recently converted sex goddess myself. I'll admit it – men are suckers for my charisma and curves. I have the best friends ever and a job girls would kill for. My magnificent shoe collection would make you gasp with pleasure. It took a bit of work on my part (and a ton of cash for the shoes), but with the mind and body makeover found in these pages plus a pinch of determination and desire, I have reached true sex goddess status. Now it's your turn.

You're about to join an elite club of women, who not only have the world at their stiletto-clad feet, but who have the guts to take that first step too...

1 Definition of a Sex Goddess

What it *really* means to earn yourself the title

Classic sex goddess characteristics

The first thing you need to know about being a sex goddess is that there's no age restriction. True, with years comes a certain confidence – you become more at ease in your own skin and have lashings of life experience – but the sparkle and recklessness of youth are just as essential.

No matter what age you are when you pick up this book, you will find something in here that relates to you and, by reading it, you'll discover an even more insanely gorgeous version of yourself inside. In order to really qualify, however, there are a handful of attributes that every goddess must have.

Confidence
She has that self-assuredness that comes from knowing she's really something special. A sex goddess is never arrogant, but she has a cocky spirit that's derived from being happy with the way she looks and proud of the person she is.

Grace
It's hard to define, but grace is the calm, serene poise that a sex goddess is blessed with. It's an elegance – the ability to be discreet and dignified. Sarah Jessica Parker, a goddess in her own right, has "grace" as the screen saver to her cell phone, just to remind herself to be good to people.

Strength
A sex goddess is brave and fearless. Even in the toughest of situations, she has the courage to remain true to herself and fight for her cause. She does not apologize for her beliefs, she does not quit and she does not let anyone, or anything, get her down.

Humor
A sex goddess can laugh at herself… and she has a beautiful laugh, whether light and twinkly or loud and uproarious. Humor gives her good perspective, strengthens her spirit, and makes her amazingly good company. Her joy is infectious and she gets a kick out of cracking everyone else up too.

"We are all of us stars and we all deserve to twinkle." Marilyn Monroe

Charm
There's nothing as enticing as a goddess who's got her game on. With her flirtatious, alluring, mesmerizing ways, she can have anyone wrapped around her little finger – but that's such a nice place to be. When a sex goddess gives you attention you feel like the sun is shining on you; nothing beats the tingling warmth of her charm.

Loyalty

Once you've found a good goddess (or she's found you) you have a friend for life. She'll defend you in an argument, never forget your birthday, let you rant and rave hysterically at her, and throw you the most fabulous parties. She'll never forget you and never let you feel unloved. Best of all – she'll turn you into a goddess too.

"You gain strength, experience, and confidence by every experience where you really stop to look fear in the face. You must do the thing you cannot do." Eleanor Roosevelt

Intelligence

Degrees and doctorates aren't necessary, but a goddess is nevertheless well-read, sharp, and knowledgeable. She can hold a good conversation, she's a great listener, and she's open-minded. She's interested and soaks up information, from popular culture to hard-core politics, and she can wax lyrical on almost any subject. If there's something she doesn't know, she's happy to admit it and determined to find out more.

It's an incredible woman that possesses all the qualities mentioned above. But the truth is, you really are something special. Even if you feel lacking in one area, time, experience, and tenacity are all you need to help polish and hone each attribute to your satisfaction. Above all, a sex goddess has a wild, vivid, irresistible spirit and that's what makes her stand out in a crowd.

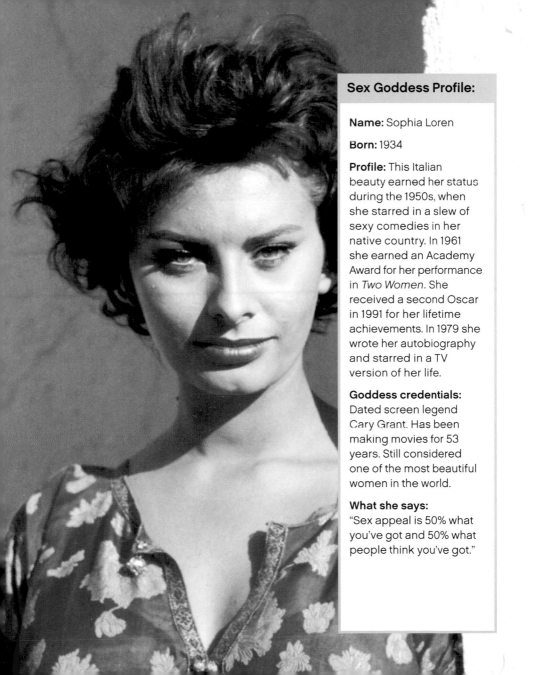

Sex Goddess Profile:

Name: Sophia Loren

Born: 1934

Profile: This Italian beauty earned her status during the 1950s, when she starred in a slew of sexy comedies in her native country. In 1961 she earned an Academy Award for her performance in *Two Women*. She received a second Oscar in 1991 for her lifetime achievements. In 1979 she wrote her autobiography and starred in a TV version of her life.

Goddess credentials: Dated screen legend Cary Grant. Has been making movies for 53 years. Still considered one of the most beautiful women in the world.

What she says: "Sex appeal is 50% what you've got and 50% what people think you've got."

The look of a goddess

Blonde, brunette, redhead? Lithe and leggy or a ton of curves? None of that matters. A sex goddess doesn't have to have a specific body type or hair color to earn her status. Girls that just ooze glamour come in all shapes and sizes. Nevertheless, there are some key features that all these women do possess.

Their hair, while being groomed, is never over-styled. Forget the hair-sprayed helmet look – a goddess's mane is more unruly (she made bed-head sexy). And her eyes have those thick sooty lashes (the kind that defy mascara) that she's perfected looking through in a sultry manner. She's totally comfortable in her own skin and she's not above flashing a little of it now and then. (She does this so casually, it's almost like she didn't mean it to happen… almost.) And her body is toned and strong – not hard-core buff, not stick-insect thin, but it definitely doesn't resemble Jell-O either.

Every goddess possesses amazing style. It's as simple as that. The clothes she chooses always manage to flatter her figure and she pulls off outfits in ways that mere mortals could never hope to achieve. Her hip-ness permeates her closet and she can suddenly make anything cool again – from vintage tweed blazers to skinny Bermuda shorts. Whether she splashes out on designer cashmere or raids her great aunt's chiffon scarves, a goddess will instantly appear the height of chic. She's equally capable of pairing leather with spiked heels and looking downright dirty, too. Famous sex goddesses, and the kind that you see on the street, all have the ability to start a trend; there's a blend of confidence and panache that helps them lead the way.

Most goddesses develop a signature style of their own. Their clothes say a lot about the women inside. Don't be surprised if the attire's a little racy; sex goddesses usually are. But demure kitten heels and a pencil skirt can give a glimpse of just as much *va-va-voom*.

Talk to a goddess, and you'll instantly adore her. It will be her combination of charm and street smarts, her wicked sense of humor and irresistible bluntness. Plus she'll be flirting with you (goddesses love to flirt). Her sex appeal is electric and she can use it to her advantage. You'll notice she's self-assured and spirited; she knows what she wants and there's no doubt she has the ways and means to get it.

You may feel a tinge of envy – how on earth can she be so confident? Does she *ever* feel low? It's good to know that sex goddesses are excellent actresses. Even when they're not feeling on top form, they'll still have a glossy veneer. They'll never wallow in sadness or disappointment – they're always looking for that silver lining.

So where can you meet a sex goddess? Women with that special *je ne sais quoi* can be found everywhere. They're in countries where women have the freedom to be powerful and equal to men. They have no inhibitions and are fearless in following their dreams. Sex goddesses often have amazing jobs, or are pursuing their goals and will achieve great things sooner or later. You can find these incredible women in every walk of life – from actresses to teachers, athletes to traders.

Having it all

Being a sex goddess is not a part-time job. It's not just about sizzling in the bedroom, or deciding to pluck your eyebrows more regularly. Once you become empowered, you can heat up every aspect of your life. What are your wildest dreams? What do you wish you could achieve at work, in your relationships, or with your body? Once your head's in the right place, everything else will follow and will fit perfectly like a magnificent, life-size jigsaw puzzle.

On the inside: you will feel more confident and ready to face new challenges. You'll be more open-minded about trying new things, like making a career change, taking a belly-dancing class or turning up at a party solo. You'll be more content with the way you look, you'll lose your hang-ups and will learn to love (instead of despise) the bits that make you different.

On the outside: you'll become a style maven! You'll wear clothes that make the most of your body in colors that look like they were made for you. You'll have fantastic hair, silky-soft skin, and you'll apply make-up like a pro. Your personality will shine through your fashion choices and women will be begging you for tips on how to look as good as you do.

In relationships: you'll be in control. You'll have the feminine wiles to snare any man you want and you'll always leave him entranced. Your romances will be long, lusty, and full of life. With your friends, you'll be loyal, loving, and generous – but you'll never be walked over.

In the bedroom: you'll always be satisfied. You can forget the sexual hang-ups – you'll know exactly what you want, how to ask for it, and how to enjoy it. You'll be just as in-tune with his body and will use that to stroke, touch, and tweak every bit of him until he can't take any more. And if things don't go according to plan? You will have the class and confidence to handle that situation too.

In your career: the sky's the limit. You'll decide what you want out of life and you'll have the drive, desire, and dash to go out and get it. Your boss will look at you differently, you'll command a new respect in the workplace, and promotions and pay rises will be yours for the taking!

2 Inside... out

Bring your sex-goddess
self to the surface

It's all in the mind

No matter what you may be thinking right now, there *is* a goddess inside you and this chapter is all about letting her out. Confidence is key, but feeling self-assured and learning to love yourself isn't always easy. The tips and suggestions over the next few pages will help change the way you feel. Performing a mind overhaul is the toughest part in the journey to sex goddess, but once you've achieved this, everything else will fall effortlessly into place.

Look at any sex goddess and you'll see she oozes confidence. She's happy to be in her skin and she has the spirit and sureness to take on new challenges, standing up to anything that's in her way. Don't be fooled into thinking that she was naturally blessed with these gifts — although it may be harder for some people to achieve than others, confidence is everyone's for the taking.

Got to have that cup of coffee *before* you step into the shower? Read magazines from back to front? Have a secret love for show tunes? These are the things that make you irresistibly unique, but you have to discover them yourself before someone else will love you for them. We constantly grow and develop as people, but are often too busy living life to sit back and acknowledge the changes. Take time out for yourself — traveling alone is the perfect way to find out what you're really about. Can't take six months for a self-discovery trip to Goa? Book a week at a yoga retreat or a beach resort and go solo. Haven't got the time or money? Take an entire day to yourself every few weeks. Decide how you want to fill the time, find out what makes you happy, and discover what makes you, *you*.

Once you realize the kind of person you are and what interests you, expand on the things you like and develop them further. You'll be far more self-assured when talking about your love for paintings, for example, if you spend time reading art magazines or visiting galleries. Plus, there's nothing more appealing than a woman who pursues her passions – from skating to knitting. It's also a great idea to subscribe to a daily or Sunday newspaper. Keeping abreast of current affairs not only widens your horizons, but gives you better control over your own thoughts and means you won't feel intimidated in social situations.

" I stand for freedom of expression, doing what you believe in, and going after your dreams."
Madonna

Use this new-found awareness of yourself and the world around you in other areas of your life. Learn how to read situations with friends or colleagues, judge your place in the group (or office) dynamic, and follow your convictions. Understand when you are truly comfortable in a situation and what makes you feel good and try to replicate this as often as you can. Try to develop a positive mental attitude – look for the good in people, the silver linings behind the dark clouds, the highlights of an otherwise bad day. Don't care too much what others think of you and don't judge yourself based on anyone else's opinion. Like yourself for who you are and don't change for anyone.

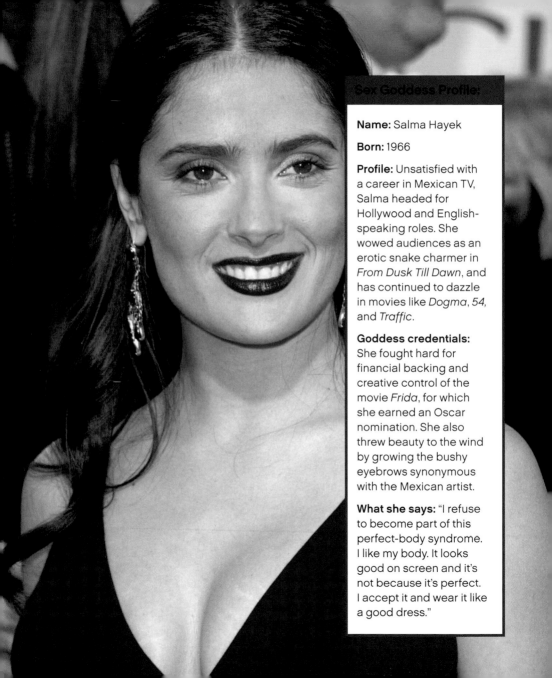

Name: Salma Hayek

Born: 1966

Profile: Unsatisfied with a career in Mexican TV, Salma headed for Hollywood and English-speaking roles. She wowed audiences as an erotic snake charmer in *From Dusk Till Dawn*, and has continued to dazzle in movies like *Dogma*, *54*, and *Traffic*.

Goddess credentials: She fought hard for financial backing and creative control of the movie *Frida*, for which she earned an Oscar nomination. She also threw beauty to the wind by growing the bushy eyebrows synonymous with the Mexican artist.

What she says: "I refuse to become part of this perfect-body syndrome. I like my body. It looks good on screen and it's not because it's perfect. I accept it and wear it like a good dress."

Right here, right now

Often our self-worth is determined by *ifs*. "If I was 5 lbs lighter I would like my body," or, "if I got a promotion I would be doing well at work." It's great to have goals, but basing your self-belief on something that may not happen is never going to make you feel like an amazing person. Instead, concentrate on the stuff going on in your life right this second that you're pleased with: "I went to the gym today," or, "I had a productive meeting with my boss."

Whenever your goals feel hard to obtain, stick to the right here, right now and focus on feeling good about what you're doing to reach them. When we need a little support, we tend to turn to those closest to us. So while on the hunt for your inner goddess, let your friends or your parents become your own pep squad. They already adore your generous nature or salty sense of humor. By reminding you of this, they'll reaffirm that you're special. Surround yourself with positive, sparkly people and let their optimism rub off on you.

When you're looking for a little guidance, find a role model. She's the woman who can work a room, pass off a Sara Lee gateau as her own, and ask her boss for a pay rise. She's got loads of confidence and watching her is like getting the whole scoop on what it's all about. Don't feel weird about asking her for advice – goddesses are always willing to share their knowledge. Ideally she'll be a few years older than you too, so she'll be able to give you some pointers from her own experience.

Treat yourself

Vogue **editor and legendary fashionista Diana Vreeland wore red. Jackie O chose oversize shades. Audrey Hepburn opted for shift dresses and ballet pumps. So how do you make the most of what you've got? Every sex goddess should have a signature style – it's like a flash of personality, a small fanfare that lets people know you've arrived.**

Your signature can be anything – maybe you have fantastic legs (in which case a miniskirt is the only way to go), you could adore magenta (so always have an accessory in this hue), or perhaps you have a fascination with chandelier earrings (collect them and wear every pair).

Decide what looks good on you, what you enjoy wearing, and embrace it. Give every outfit a twist, make it personal, *own* your clothes. Your signature doesn't have to be expensive, either. Say you covet vintage bags; scour flea markets to find the right pieces to match your outfits. They're usually cheaper than anything you'd find in a department store and you can be sure no one else will have them.

Everybody loves to be spoiled – especially a sex goddess. But don't sit around waiting for that bouquet of long-stemmed flowers or the bottle of Dom Perignon to land on your doorstep, take the matter into your own hands and show yourself some affection. Make your love gifts regular (once a week should do) and big or small depending on your budget. Sometimes splurging out on a grand caramel macchiato at Starbucks is all it takes. Other times a weekend away could be in order. You'll soon discover what constitutes a pick-me-up and you'll know when you deserve that extra something special. Reward yourself even if you're not feeling blue – pampering shouldn't just be reserved for down days – boost your self-worth and celebrate just being you.

Budget

The new paperback by your favorite author.

A bottle of nail polish in an eye-popping hue.

Coffee and a flaky pastry from a fancy French patisserie.

An apple martini in a swanky bar straight after work.

A bunch of mauve tulips.

A taxi home from *anywhere*.

Blowout

A pair of Manolo Blahniks that weren't on sale.

A St. Tropez tan at an upscale beauty salon.

Dinner at the poshest restaurant in town.

A weekend in a faraway city.

Vintage jewelry.

A bottle of champagne with no good reason to drink it.

Faking it

Take the fast track – make everyone believe you're already the sassiest, sexiest goddess before you've even got there. Sure, inside you may feel like a quivering bag of nerves, but nobody else has to know that. Do your best Catherine Zeta Jones-at-the-Oscars impression – act like you totally belong.

You can fake it a number of ways:

* Act as naturally as possible, but be subtle about it – try too hard to be someone you're not and you'll blow your cover. Follow other people's lead from the smallest things like what to drink, to what to talk about or wear. The best way to appear to fit in is to become one of the pack. Once you've developed the nerve, then you can let your sex goddess wildness shine through.

* Alternatively, show off your acting skills and play the most confident, gorgeous, feisty version of yourself (remember the way you feel in your sexiest outfit after a heady glass of champagne) and replicate. Pretend you're this luscious lady and no one will know you're a fraud. They'll respond to your faux aplomb and will figure you were just born bold.

* Dress to dazzle and, instead of sloping into a room, strut. Look people in the eye when you talk to them, then laugh at their jokes, and flirt outrageously. Be calm, stand tall, accept a compliment gracefully – do all the things you know a sex goddess would do. Remember, practice makes perfect, so try this routine a few times and soon it will feel like second nature. After a while you won't even be faking fearlessness… you'll be the real deal.

Sex Goddess Profile:

Name: Audrey Hepburn

Born: 1929

Profile: Suffered depression and malnutrition in Nazi-occupied Holland during the Second World War, but pulled through. She attended ballet school and modeled, then finally broke into movies and garnered praise for classics like *My Fair Lady*, *Roman Holiday*, and, of course *Breakfast at Tiffany's*.

Goddess credentials: Her sleek, chic style, poise, and grace have made her a fashion icon and she continues to influence women the world over.

What she says: "I know I have more sex appeal on the tip of my nose than many people have in their entire bodies. It doesn't stand out a mile, but it's there."

3 Feeling Hot, Looking Hotter

How to see a goddess when
you look in the mirror

Shape up

Who's *totally* happy with her body? Seriously? How many celebrity interviews have you read where a seemingly stunning, crazily thin woman is complaining about how she doesn't always feel beautiful or that there are parts of her body that need improving? It's insane. Time and again this proves that, no matter how tall, short, thin, or fat a girl may be, she can be unhappy with herself. Surely it would be better to *love* your figure and celebrate its size and shape – whatever it may be.

"We can be beautiful at all ages. Feminine beauty comes in all shapes, sizes, colors, ways."
Lauren Hutton

Flick through any fashion magazine and you're bound to get a little depressed by the constant images of jutting hipbones, perky breasts, and mile-long legs. But who really looks like that and why does your own body image have to mirror it? The first step to embracing your own figure is to stop comparing it to the airbrushed images you see in magazines or on TV.

Work it

Let's face it – most of us are more J. Lo than Gisele when it comes to body shape. We have curves that are never going to go away (and why should we want them to?), but that doesn't mean we can't make them more toned and luscious. Apart from making you stronger, fitter, and healthier, exercise is a great way to improve your body image.

For a start, when you exercise, your body releases endorphins into your blood stream, which enhance that feel-good factor. Secondly, when you start paying attention to how fit or strong you are, you stop thinking about how your body *looks* and focus instead on what your body can *do*.

The leotard and legwarmers were heinous, but Olivia Newton-John did get something right when she sang her 1981 hit. We should – get physical, that is – every day. That doesn't mean hard-core aerobics sessions or even pumping iron at the gym 24/7, but it does mean being active and raising your heart rate for at least 30 minutes a day. Walking or hiking outside is great, as are cycling, swimming, even your half hour grinding on a dance floor. Becoming a gym bunny is a good way to motivate yourself, especially if you work it into your daily routine by always attending certain classes. Keep yourself on the straight and narrow by getting a friend to sign up too – it's a lot harder to make excuses and take off early for a glass of wine when she's already practicing her yoga stretches.

Bite me

Goddesses do not diet. It's tedious, depressing, and rarely works – 95% of dieters regain the weight they lose in one to five years. Plus, there's nothing fun about restraining yourself from food you *really* want to eat. But, just as you're unlikely to see a sex goddess turn down dessert, you'll also not see her polishing off an entire pint of Ben & Jerry's. Eating any food in moderation is okay.

Most women base their self-worth on how good their body looks and how "well" they've eaten that day. But a goddess knows that defining food as good or evil is like hitching the bus to Bluesville. Instead of deciding how certain foods make you feel *emotionally*, focus on how they make you feel *physically*. Does a bacon cheeseburger make you feel nauseous? Do you feel bloated after a huge plate of pasta? Do you crave chocolate just 20 minutes after you've eaten mashed potatoes? Notice how eating starches (white bread, pasta, potatoes, and rice) late in the evening makes you feel heavy and uncomfortable, even harder to sleep, while leafy green vegetables, like spinach, or proteins, like chicken or fish, leave you full without feeling gross and overstuffed. Make your dietary choices based on what tastes good but also on foods that leave you refueled and energized.

If you do want to get slimmer, make sure you do it sensibly. Fad and food exclusion diets are definitely not the way to go. From the Atkins diet to the raw-foods diet, to the blood-type diet, to the cabbage-soup diet, the truth is, no matter how much weight you lose digesting these bizarre food combinations, you'll put it all back on again once you go back to your regular eating habits.

Snack attack

It's 3pm and, whether you're bored or hungry, you have those junk-food cravings. Shun chocolate bars and chips in favor of these nibbles, which are just as instant but are healthier and should curb your appetite too. Choose one thing from each category to make up a smart snack.

Group one

Low-fat popcorn
Trail mix
An apple
Fig bars
Box of raisins
Half a banana
Hummus and pita bread

Group two

Hard-boiled egg whites
Level tablespoon of peanut butter
Five almonds
Fat-free yogurt

The only way to lose fat is to burn off more calories than you consume. So, to lose pounds the healthy way, combine exercise and good eating habits. The best way to drop weight is to have four small meals and two snacks throughout the day. This will keep your metabolism at a constant and stop you from feeling hungry. In every meal balance complex carbohydrates like fibrous vegetables and whole grains with lean protein like fish, turkey, and chicken. Each portion of food (protein or carbs) should not be bigger than the surface area of the palm of your hand (one of the biggest mistakes we make is with portion control).

Steer clear of starches, junk food, and alcohol. Don't aim to, or expect to, lose more than 2 lbs a week, or the chances are very high that you'll regain this weight. See healthy eating as a way of life – once you have reached your desired weight, stick to the same healthy foods you've been consuming but allow yourself a treat once in a while. Remember, you'll pile the pounds back on if you resort to a daily menu of burger and fries. Dieting should not make you miserable, so if you're having real problems with yo-yo eating plans see a nutritionist for even more solid advice. The other thing to keep in mind is, if you combine diet and exercise, you may not notice a big weight loss on the scales as muscle (which you should be building by exercising) weighs more than fat. Throw out your scales and judge your progress on how your clothes fit instead.

Be good to yourself

A sex goddess knows how to have a wild time. She'll be the first person to order champagne, the last person to leave the dance floor, and the only one to suggest doing it all over again the following week. But she'll also cancel her plans so she can snuggle up under a cashmere blanket and rent black-and-white movies all weekend if she needs to. A sex goddess is totally in touch with herself – mind, body, and soul – so even though she's bursting out of a birthday cake in a lamé bikini one minute (figuratively speaking), she acknowledges when she has to take things down a notch and give herself a chance to recharge.

The den of Zen: who hasn't gone a little overboard on the booze, cigarettes, and drugs at some point in her life (or the last few weeks)? Such nights are hazy memories at best, while the mornings are hell on earth. Chances are, during every hangover you vow never to drink again, and yet the promise is broken the moment a martini is placed in front of you. No matter how cool blowing smoke rings may look, every sex goddess knows cigarette breath, nicotine-tinted teeth, and smoke-scented hair are disgusting. And alcohol may be a great icebreaker, but getting so trashed you're out of control is foul. To avoid becoming drunk and undesirable, drink a glass of water between every alcoholic beverage (fool friends into thinking it's a vodka and tonic) and try to limit yourself to one cigarette every hour (instead of one every five minutes).

Get some shut-eye: call it beauty sleep, growing time, or a good rest. Whatever it is, your body needs it. Eight hours sleep a night is a great way to look and feel gorgeous in the morning. Don't get enough and your skin, digestive system, mental alertness, physical energy, and entire well being will be messed up. So find your eye mask and retire to your boudoir this instant.

Sun sinners: while there's no denying a tan makes you look like a slimmer, healthier, more gorgeous version of yourself, the risk of developing skin cancer means it's so much safer to fake than bake. Get the goddess look with a sunless tanning cream instead (if you can't handle DIY, visit one of the spray-on tanning booths which are popping up in salons everywhere). If you have to step out into the sun, only do so once you've covered yourself with at least a shot-glass worth of SPF 15 or higher and reapply every two hours. Floppy hats and huge shades are so Italian Riviera and make great sunshades too.

Stress-fest: every high-flying, fast-paced woman is going to get a little stressed-out; it can't be helped. When you're juggling a job, a relationship, a social life, a fitness regime, future goals, and everything else that goes along with being young, hip, and on your way up, you're bound to freak out at times. Reduce the tension, anxiety, and insomnia by learning how to plan your time better, by creating space for yourself (this is where the cashmere blanket and old-movie renting come in) and by accepting that every ball can be dropped a few times. Life does go on.

Keep it real: the girl who will only drink water, eat raw carrot sticks, make gym dates, be in bed by 10pm, and slathers on SPF 45 every time she leaves the house is no fun to hang out with. She's not a sex goddess. The girl who indulges in the odd frozen margarita, can beat you in a running race, and is proud of her round, swingy breasts is as sexy as hell.

Perfectly polished

Notice how you always feel good after a visit to the hair salon? You can be wearing your most unbecoming top and your baggiest sweatpants, but if your hair looks great, your skin glows and you feel like a million dollars. It's the same with a manicure. A French polish or a slick of Chanel Rouge Noir can turn a plain old T-shirt and jeans into a classy ensemble. The crazy thing is, most women see a trip to the salon to get someone else to blow-dry their hair or paint their nails as a frivolous luxury.

A sex goddess, on the other hand, knows this is essential grooming. What's the point in splashing out on a pair of strappy heels, only to accessorize them with hard skin and battered toenails? And why spend an hour perfecting your eye shadow, only to top it off with fuzzy, unruly brows? Start putting aside maintenance money and scheduling weekly salon visits. If this still seems extravagant, justify it with any of the following reasons.

You'll look good: shiny hair, polished nails, shaped brows, and stubble-free legs are the added extras that make you that bit glossier and better groomed. They'll also come in handy when you bump into your ex-boyfriend in the grocery store, or an old college acquaintance at the movies. Don't save looking your best *just* for that big party or a wedding, make it an everyday occurrence.

You'll feel good: you already know that when you feel confident inside you glow on the outside, so look at grooming as your secret ammo. Catch a glimpse of your recently highlighted hair in the mirror and it could be the thing that stops you crawling miserably back into bed in the morning, refusing to face the world.

You'll enjoy doing it: reclining in a comfy chair while somebody else pampers, primps, and preens you – what's not to love?

Budget

Buy an at-home French manicure kit. It contains two shades of polish and stickers to place on your nails to help get those perfect white tips.

Blowout

Go to a salon for your French manicure. Get a pedicure while you're at it (amazing with open-toe sandals). Tip: Make your polish last longer by applying a clear top coat every other day.

Touch-me hair: there's no *one* style that every sex goddess should have, but there *is* one thing they all have in common – the kind of hair you can't resist running your fingers through. Desirable tresses are glossy, healthy, and a tiny bit unruly (*au revoir* straight-laced chignons). The other important thing to remember is to have a distinct style. Whether it's platinum blonde with a blunt fringe, a side-swept part with face-framing layers, or a messy, pixie crop – your cut should be bold, not blah. Find one of the best hairstylists in your city and pay him or her a visit. It may feel like a lot of money, but remember this is something you wear *every* day. Do it... because you're worth it.

Kiss and make up: smoky, come-to-bed eyes, or glossy lick-me lips? The choice is yours, but you can only have one, because playing up both features is overkill and just not hot. By day, keep it simple with a dab of concealer and a dusting of bronzer, but when night falls, shake things up a little. Decide whether you'll draw attention to eyes or lips. If it's eyes, smudge a charcoal shade over your lids, or take style cues from the 1960s and apply a pastel color wash with a sweep of black liquid eyeliner. Take a walk on the wild side with fake eyelashes (the individual lashes are harder to apply but the end result is worth the effort). For lips, make them matte or glossy and choose any shade from poppy to peony. Never, *ever* line your lips with a dark pencil and fill with a lighter shade (so not sexy) and, while on the subject, leave the glitter, stick-on jewels, and temporary tattoos to the kids too.

Name: Cindy Crawford

Born: 1966

Profile: One of the original supermodels, Cindy's face has graced over 600 magazine covers from *Vogue* to *Playboy*. She's had a film career, has presented MTV's *House of Style*, is author of a makeup manual, and has produced a slew of work-out videos.

Goddess credentials: Cindy has a multi-million-dollar career, two beautiful kids, an entrepreneur husband, Rande Gerber, and one of the hottest ranked bodies in the world. Who says you can't have it all?

What she says: "I think women see me on the cover of magazines and think I never have a pimple or bags under my eyes. But that's after two hours of hair and makeup, plus retouching. Even I don't wake up looking like Cindy Crawford."

Body language

Now we've established that your body is actually gorgeous, it's time to discover the best way to show it off. This means highlighting those extra special bits and diverting attention away from those less-than-perfect areas. The best way to do this is by using the tricks of a fashionista's trade – cut and color. Highlighted below are some of the simple rules to follow, depending on your body shape, and it's definitely worth taking yourself out for a mammoth shopping trip to try on everything and anything which will help you determine which styles work best for you. Once you've found the cuts and shapes that most flatter your figure you can base your entire wardrobe around them. If you want to avoid fashion faux pas before you've even made them, remember that learning what doesn't suit you is just as important, and this applies to fabrics as well as the cut of a garment.

Color is key – no matter how classy beige may be, if it washes out your skin, it will never look elegant. For a sex goddess, skin is always in, but try and avoid the obvious – legs and cleavage will turn heads, but show something unexpected and temperatures will really soar. Try highlighting the curve of your back, your collarbone, or exposing your neck instead.

Once you know exactly what suits you, you can start experimenting with each season's trends by adapting items to fit your look and only buying clothes in cuts that suit you. If the shapes are simply wrong for you, keep your clothes classic and incorporate hip accessories into your look instead (this is a much cheaper way of staying fashion forward too).

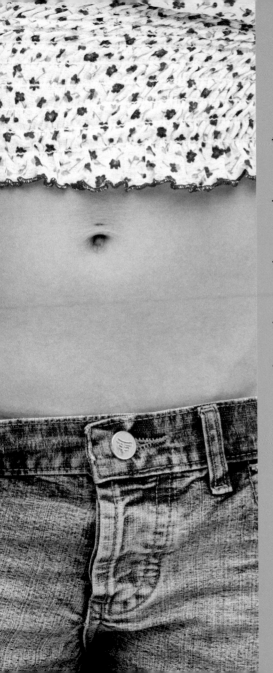

Hourglass

* Embrace your curves with slim-fitting clothes that show off your waist, as well as your bust.

* Scoop-neck tops accentuate your decolletage. Avoid high necks – they look better with a small bust.

* Flat-fronted pants keep you streamlined and a boot cut balances your figure.

* Low-rise pants that sit on your hips are also a perfect fit for you.

* Rather than hiding your shape under layers of chunky fabric, stick to light flowing fabrics like silk that will skim over your body instead of hiding it, or wear clothes with more structure.

* Dazzle with accessories on your skinniest body parts, like bangles on your wrists, dangling chandeliers on your earlobes, and jeweled thongs on your feet.

* Choose longer-lined jackets and Burberry-style macs and pair these with slim-fit, tailored dresses or light camisoles and dark denim jeans.

Petite

* Add virtual inches to your height by dressing in one color and wearing high heels, but don't overdo the height. Slingbacks are a good option.

* You look great in patterns and frills so choose tops with adornment. Because you have a small frame be careful not to break up the line of your clothes with belts or short skirts.

* A fluid silhouette is very flattering (a simple, one-color dress would achieve this).

Pear shaped

* Wear darker colors on the bottom half of your body to slim it down and draw attention upward.

* Patterns, frills, corsages, and adornments look fantastic – but on your top half only.

* A wide, boat-neck top will balance your curvy hips and bottom.

* Avoid full, circle skirts that make hips look bigger, stick to a pencil skirt or long boot-leg pants.

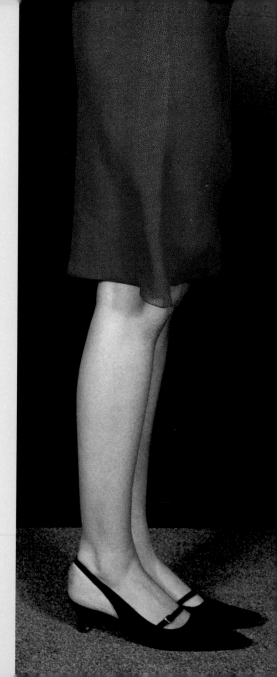

Tall and leggy

* Create the illusion of curves by choosing pieces that belt or tie around your waist.

* Break up long legs with capri pants or pencil skirts and heels with ankle straps.

* Horizontal stripes are adorable and you can pull them off with aplomb.

* If you're proud of your pins, there's nothing sexier than a mini, but keep your shoes flat to avoid looking trashy.

Large tummy

* Wear light gauzy shirts or dresses with an empire line, which fit under your bust then skim over your stomach.

* Direct the focus onto your fabulous legs by wearing a baggier shirt (to cover your waist) over a miniskirt (to show off the pins).

* Invest in underwear with a stomach control panel to flatten your figure – perfect worn under a dress and so much simpler than breathing in!

* Don't tuck in your shirt or wear anything belted or cropped at the waist – move your accessories higher up and wear a wide-necked top with cool earrings, a chunky necklace, or a chiffon scarf tied Grace-Kelly style.

More dash than cash?

Dressing like you've just stepped off a catwalk doesn't have to cost a supermodel's salary. A sex goddess is as savvy as she is stylish and she knows that there are ways to get the look she wants without having to survive on ramen noodles for the rest of the month.

Take a long, hard look at your closet and gather together everything you haven't worn in the last two years. Organize a stoop or garage sale; keep your prices low and people will flock.

Log onto ebay, the Internet auction site. This is a great place to sell unwanted designer items (the more covetable the piece, the higher price it will fetch). Alternatively, if there's something you've been obsessing over, this could be the place to find it – at a much cheaper rate. Beware when bidding though – don't bother placing your bid until 10 minutes before an auction ends (or you'll probably get outbid and will just push up the price) and make sure that you don't get caught up in a bidding frenzy, so spending more than you wanted to.

Consignment, goodwill, and thrift stores are great places to hunt for stylish items with rock-bottom price tags. Get friendly with the owners and they'll put aside things that you might want. The neighborhood in which the shop is situated often reflects the quality of clothes you'll find inside, so check out goodwill stores in up-market areas for designer clothes that have barely been worn. If you don't like the idea of buying second-hand clothes, stick to accessories like bags, scarves, and costume jewelry.

10 essential sex goddess items

Oversize sunglasses
Can you say Jackie O? Slipping on a pair of shades is like adding instant glamour to any outfit. Avoid wearing indoors or on a rainy day – there is such a thing as trying too hard.

Butt-defying jeans
Every girl has a gazillion pairs in her closet, but you should only wear to death the ones that make your thighs look slimmer and your butt smaller.

Amazing coat
Think of all the cash you spend on great clothes, only to cover them with the same old black winter coat. Invest in a hip overcoat in a unique color – a pink dogtooth check, a camel herringbone, or a simple cream wool. Pay attention to interesting details like a belt, leather piping, or oversize pockets. You can keep the clothes underneath simple and let your overcoat show off your supreme sense of style.

Slinky dress
Choose something in silk or jersey that clings to your curves. It doesn't have to be black, but you'll get more mileage out of a dark color, so try chocolate or charcoal gray instead. This should be the kind of dress that you can slip on for an impromptu dinner with killer heels, or wear after a day at the beach with leather flip-flops and tousled hair.

Killer heels

Strappy sandals with skinny heels
jazz up a pair of jeans and turn
a pencil skirt or slip dress into a
dynamite ensemble. Tip: Make
sure you can walk in them; there's
nothing wrong with heels so
towering that they'll only take you
as far as the first taxi, but you must
also have a pair that can be worn
on the dance floor.

Clutch bag
A good day bag is vital, but when it comes to nighttime you have to switch things up a bit. A clutch bag always looks chic and, conveniently, you can hold it under you arm, keeping your hands free for more important things, like drinks. Choose a neutral shade that will either match or contrast nicely with most of your outfits – consider matte silver or gold as both these work well with most colors.

Figure-flattering bikini

Easier said than done. Be prepared to try on a ton of different styles because the one that you expect to be least flattering could actually be the opposite. When you've found a swimsuit that you really do feel good in, buy more than one – a sex goddess knows there are far more enjoyable things to do on the beach than worry about how her butt/belly/boobs are looking.

Diamonds

They're every girl's best friend but they don't have to cost the earth. Check out antique fairs for good prices on small diamond trinkets and, if your budget really doesn't stretch that far, buy a small pair of Cubic Zircona earrings and, if anyone asks, lie (the smaller they are, the more convincing this will be!).

Cashmere sweater

Classic, comfortable, and timeless. Wear it with a suit to work, with a leather skirt for an evening out, and with your jeans when you're chilling. Start off with a simple style and color, like a black crew or roll nock, and then build your collection.

Expensive watch

You wear it every day, so make an investment and see how it increases the value of your entire outfit. Buy something simple that complements the rest of your wardrobe and you'll be glad you did – a classic silver Gucci watch will turn your look from girl to goddess every day of the week.

Something simply amazing

Every now and again you will see something gorgeous that you can't live without. It will take your breath away. It will evoke visions of you sitting on a yacht in Monte Carlo wearing it, or attending a New York Gala with it tied around your neck (or feet if you're salivating through the window at Manolo Blahnik). When you see this wonderful thing, you shouldn't hold back, but live out your fashion fantasies instead, even if it's only once a year.

These beautiful, expensive things are the items you'll care for and covet for years to come. These are the things that you'll pass on to your grandchildren. When you buy, don't give in to the guilt (unless your credit card is maxed, in which case you should probably ignore this bit), but enjoy every second of the pandering sales assistant, the crisp logoed tissue paper, the glazed shopping bag. For almost all sex goddesses (except the mega-rich) these moments are few and far between, which is why they should be savored and most definitely indulged.

If you've read this entire chapter and decided none of it is relevant to you because you simply don't have the occasion or environment to care too much about style – think again! There are no excuses for living your life in tapered jeans and faded sweatshirts, or for wearing your hair scraped back in a ponytail every day. Don't just dress for yourself or your friends, dress for the girl that glances over admiringly on the train every morning, and the guy in the deli, and all the other random people who pass you in the street and think to themselves, "Wow, she looks amazing." Dress to impress everyone – always. It's what a sex goddess does.

4 Secrets of
Seduction

How to find yourself a sex god and make him melt

It's a guy thing

What kind of man does a sex goddess date? He has to be charming, confident, witty, and intelligent. He has to be wildly attractive (to you anyway) and whenever you're near him you should feel an insatiable urge to rip his clothes off and have wild sex with him right then and there. Yet, despite his erotic allure, he should also be a gentleman – a sex goddess doesn't have a problem with being bought flowers, taken out for dinner, or even having a door held open for her once in a while.

He should also appreciate your own wit and wiliness and see you as an equal. Above all he should adore you, not in a patronizing puppy-dog way, but in the way that he knows you're always the most gorgeous woman in the room and he's lucky to be with you.

And whenever he's with you he's laughing at your jokes, marveling at your knowledge, and fantasizing about peeling off your underwear, all at once.

Okay, all this might seem a lot to ask for – charm, brains, and killer good looks all in one package? That is a rare treat. Looking for the perfect guy means having relationships with a few flawed ones along the way – and that's part of the fun of it. The truth is, no one is going to be everything you want at every moment of your life. Keeping high expectations is a good thing, but throwing in a pinch of reality is even better.

"I prefer ordinary girls – you know, college students, waitresses, that sort of thing. Most of the girls I go out with start as good friends." Leonardo di Caprio

The key thing to remember when dating is finding a guy that you dig. When a man approaches you in a bar, chats you up, and then asks you on a date, it can be very flattering and hard to turn down. But the next thing you know, you're stuck having dinner with someone you have nothing in common with – and certainly don't expect to be getting frisky with – just because he asked you.

Rule number one is remember number one – it's all about you.

Desperately seeking a sex god...

So where do you find this rare hunk of near perfect manliness? Surely he can't be the guy sitting next to you on your morning commute, or the man flicking through the bestsellers beside you in the bookstore? Maybe he is. Finding the right guy should be fun, not a depressing, deplorable pursuit. It's a good idea to accept now that you may kiss a few frogs before finding that prince, but if a "frog" happens to be a gorgeous European tourist who needs someone to show him the sights (and in exchange will help you perfect the art of French kissing), maybe you should suffer a little for romance!

A sex goddess *loves* men, she *loves* to date, and she *loves* having a few great stories to share at the end of it all. So keep your eyes open and follow the fizzle. If you catch a guy's eye and feel a sexual friction, or you find him so attractive that you have to concentrate on listening to him, instead of just imagining him naked, or he just makes you laugh and laugh – it's worth pursuing a date. There's nothing wrong with going after what you want – men love strong, driven women and, by making the first move yourself, you'll avoid the syndrome mentioned on the previous page, where you date guys you're not even into just because they asked you out.

When you're eyeing up potential partners, there are lots of places to check out. Bars and clubs are an obvious choice, but the loud music means your opinion will be based mostly on their appearance and dancing skills. Nevertheless, thanks to a few cocktails, this is often when you're at your least inhibited so your slay-him outfit and ragga-style grinding could really pay off!

You want to hang out with a guy with similar interests to you, so start looking in the places you frequent most – the gym, a tennis club, your favorite pool hall, the theater that shows art-house films. Equally, set-ups through friends are always worth pursuing. They're like a more trustworthy matchmaking service (without the yearly membership fee).

Feel hot, hot, hot

Before you head out for a night of sex (or light flirtation) in the city, you need to remember your goddess status. Hopefully, by now you should be feeling pretty good about yourself. Over the past few chapters you've developed confidence and self-assuredness, you've accepted your body (and hopefully even decided it's damn sexy), and you know how to look your best. Think of all this as your honey – men will buzz around you simply because you're giving off happy, sassy, sexy vibes.

Prepare for an evening out by putting on your favorite outfit – the one that you *know* makes you look amazing. Spend a little extra time getting ready – don't rush – it's important that you're feeling as hot as hell on the inside, so you can project it.

When you get to the bar, or club, think about the way you stand or sit, notice how you interact with everyone else. The worst thing you can do is sit in the corner of the bar with your head drooped, trying not to catch anyone's eye and looking miserable, or feeling awkward. The best thing you can do is sit tall, or even better stand (it's easier to feel empowered and confident). Smile a lot, look friendly and approachable. Catch people's attention, exchange a joke with the barman when you buy drinks, enjoy feeling people's eyes on you. Bask in the admiring glances, relax and savor the attention. Chat with your friends, but keep an eye on the males surrounding you. They will approach – there's no doubt. And when they do, it's time to really work the magic… which brings us to flirting.

How to flirt – a crash course

For a sex goddess, flirting is like breathing – it's second nature. Once learnt, it's a technique that you can use time and again to get what you want from any situation. Master flirting to perfection, and you will be able to ensnare any guy you like, for as long as you want him.

The most wonderful thing about flirting is that the whole process of making an amazing guy feel good about himself by flattering, enchanting, and simply letting him know that you find him attractive, will inevitably get you feeling downright gorgeous yourself. All guys respond to flirting by reciprocating, which makes for a mutual love fest. So while you're working to make him feel special, he's reacting by switching on his own charm.

Before you know it you're both feeling like a million dollars, which simply adds to the sexual attraction and is bound to end with one of you asking for a date. Sounds blissful doesn't it? And it is so easy to master flirting. It's just a simple combination of three essential ingredients – body language, sassy chat, and confidence – all executed with a dollop of good humor. Once you've got these basic aspects skillfully covered, the world is your oyster.

Here are some tame (and some downright saucy) techniques that have already helped some sex goddesses seal the deal.

* Pay his appearance a compliment – avoid the cheesy (and obvious) "do you work out?" and draw attention to his great shoes, slick haircut, or cool watch instead.

* Hold his gaze for a few seconds longer than necessary.

* Touch him "emphatically" when you talk to him (the thigh or waist are hot spots and show that you're doing more than just making your point).

* Find an excuse to flash some skin. Innocently show him the scar you received, aged 13, during hockey practice – which just happens to be on your thigh/shoulder/hip.

* Whisper in his ear – this is easy to do if you're in a noisy bar, harder if you're somewhere quiet. Tell him a secret and you're doubling the intimacy.

* Talk about something sensual, like how you prefer to sleep naked or that a massage turns you on.

* Give him a kiss on the lips when saying hello or goodbye. A light peck can be excused as a casual gesture, though you both know it's anything but.

* In a busy environment, invade his personal space slightly – the closer you stand, the more obvious your motive. When you're just millimeters away he'll have no doubt of your intentions.

The pick-up

Forget waiting for a guy to notice you. Sex goddesses don't have the time or patience. If they've seen something they want, they'll go out and get it. Here, a few real goddesses tell us how they did it.

"When the guy I liked told me he wanted to bleach his hair I offered my services. I'd never colored anyone's hair before, but that was irrelevant. I made him take his shirt off (so it wouldn't get bleached) and that combined with wet, soapy skin and intimate contact meant it wasn't long before we were making out." **Susan**

"In a bar recently, I bought a guy a drink, dropped it off with him and said, 'Hi. I don't want to interrupt your evening, but here's your next drink on me, and if you'd like to join us, we're sitting over there.' He came right over." **Dena**

"I recruited my current boyfriend for my street hockey team. Being the captain gave me the chance to pluck him from an opposing team and convince him to join us instead. I was already on a power trip then, so it was easy to take the next step and ask him out." **Rebecca**

"I got talking to a guy at a bar one summer and invited him to my annual barbeque fiesta the following weekend. I had no plans to throw a party, but after he said yes, I had to. I spent a fortune and hosted this major soirée. Luckily he did show up, and he never discovered the party was thrown for him and him alone." **Sophie**

Sex Goddess Profile:

Name: Marilyn Monroe

Born: 1926

Profile: Norma Jean Baker spent most of her childhood in foster homes. She appeared in a few movies previous, but it was the 1953 classic *Gentlemen Prefer Blondes* that launched her career. Movies like *The Seven Year Itch* and *Some Like It Hot* helped Marilyn reach iconic status. A suspected drug overdose in 1962 meant she would remain an enigma forever.

Goddess credentials: She appeared on the first ever cover of *Playboy* and was never afraid to play up to her sex-goddess status. A rumored affair with John F. Kennedy made Marilyn even more of a movie legend.

What she says: "I'm not interested in money, I just want to be wonderful."

Sizzling sex goddess dates

Not ready for the sex bit yet? Bowl him over with your classy seduction skills by suggesting one of these dates – dinner and a movie has never looked so average.

Brunch: choose a classy, old-school hotel. It's more affordable and less contrived than a dinner date, plus there's nothing sexier than getting tipsy on mimosas before midday. Who knows when you'll need to book a room?

A Day at the races: another perfect excuse to wear a hat. Be his lucky charm or throw a little cash on a filly of your choice. Drown your loser's blues at the bar or celebrate your winnings with a quickie by the stables.

Boating on a lake: lie back and let him do the work. Falling in the water isn't essential, but if the weather's warm, it's the perfect excuse to drop anchor and "sunbathe" while your clothes dry off.

Salsa night: don your heels and a ruffled skirt. Split a jug of sangria. Feel the heat of his body pressed against yours while you step forward, back, and cha-cha-cha.

A Picnic in the country: pack a hamper and take a drive, find a grassy meadow, lay out a blanket, and treat your man to strawberries and champagne – and perhaps a frolic in the fields.

Sledging: embrace your inner child and go whizzing down a powder-covered hill together on a sledge. Finish with a snowball fight (don't let him win), an icy make-out session, and hot toddies by the fire to warm up.

Roof-top cocktails: slip into a black minidress and shimmy up to the top of your roof (or that of a friend if yours is too precarious). Enjoy a glittering nighttime view of your city while you drink martinis together.

A Private box at the opera: dress like a 1920s socialite (gloves are essential). Resist his advances – at least until the lights go down.

His place or yours

You've had an amazing night together, have shared a few bottles of wine, one or two naughty secrets and a few lusty gazes. What's next? There's nothing wrong with inviting him back for a night cap – but it's good to set the boundaries right from the start. Given half the chance, men will usually be through the door and on your sofa quicker than a tom cat in spring. How long they stay is your choice.

If you definitely don't plan on having sex with this guy, let him know right away that this really is just going to be a Cointreau and coffee affair. Putting the parameters out there early on means you won't feel pressured later. If you do crave some casual sex, that's fine too, but be savvy about it – never go back to a guy's apartment if you've only just met him. Instead go back to your place. If you have a roommate, let them know, or if you're leaving your friends at a bar, get one of them to call you in 30 minutes time. It may ruin those first throes of foreplay, but so much better to be safe than sorry.

If first-night sex is unappealing (because there are still some ladies among us), keep him hanging on with the promise of what's to come. Give it all up on the first date and you have nothing left to tease him with. Play a little hard to get and you'll pique his desire, and leave him desperate to see you again.

5 In the Bedroom

Sex and the goddess

Too sexy?

There's no such thing. Being a goddess means being in touch with your emotions – all of them – right down to your deepest, darkest, dirtiest desires. Confidence in bed is just as important as in the other aspects of your life – but it's sometimes harder to gain because it is such a sensitive area. You're stripped bare (literally and figuratively) and your emotions (and breasts) are totally revealed. This is a vulnerable position to be in and it takes a pretty sassy lady to feel at ease and take control.

It's no surprise that women reach their sexual peak in their mid thirties – it takes that long to feel okay about your body and to sleep with enough guys to a) know what you're doing and b) know what you want *him* to be doing. But, as a sex goddess, you don't have to wait until you hit the big three-0 before becoming a minx in the sack. With experimentation and assertiveness you could get everything you want (including that mind-blowing orgasm) right now.

One of the biggest blows to a women's sexual confidence is her body image. You may accept your body enough to wear a killer outfit, but what about when it's time to shed the threads? The most important thing to remember is that men *love* women's bodies. When you're thinking small boobs, he's thinking pert breasts; when you're panicking about saddlebag hips, he's greedily running his eyes over your curves; when you're trying to avoid highlighting the cellulite on your butt, he's trying to caress your perfectly-formed posterior. By the time you're naked, a man's eyes are glazed over with lust. Just remember that he's viewing you in soft focus and let your worries blur away.

"God gave women intuition and femininity. Used properly, the combination easily jumbles the brain of any man I've ever met." Farrah Fawcett

Sex is not about how your body looks from a certain angle, it's about what turns you on and makes you feel good, what sends sensations through your body and how hot you can get, when the lights go out (or stay on, either way). No matter what anyone else says, loving sex and wanting lots of it is totally healthy; you should enjoy that orgasm – you deserve it. So stop thinking about it and get on with doing it.

Create a sex den

It might just take one night before you indulge in a mad sex marathon, or maybe you've been holding out for a few dates, making him crave you even more. Whatever the situation, sooner or later you'll probably be letting a man into your boudoir. But who can get horny when surrounded by dirty washing, smelly sneakers, and harsh overhead lighting?

Prepare your lair for a night of passion by setting the right atmosphere. Start by clearing away the clutter, then focus on creating coziness. Ignore the ceiling light in favor of more flattering lamps and candles (not too many though, or it may look like a séance). Choose a warm color for your sheets – burgundy or chocolate brown are good picks – and add a scattering of small cushions (useful for propping up hips, heads, and other body parts). Music is a great mood enhancer so a stereo with a remote control and an assortment of slinky CDs are a good investment. A gorgeous cut-glass decanter filled with water for quenching that mid-sex thirst is the perfect final flourish.

Once you've brought a guy back to your place, you can turn your seduction up a notch. Now it's not about cutesy ways to let him know you're interested, but more about teasing, tantalizing, and turning him on so he'll do just about anything for a piece of you. Being romantic and coy is great on a date, but this is your chance to get down and dirty and show him the real woman inside. See the next chapter for the lowdown on taking things further still – from perfecting your own sex skills to receiving that to-die-for orgasm (no vibrator necessary).

Budget

Part with a little cash for a basic full-length mirror from a DIY home store. Place it at the end of the bed in prime position to view your sexual antics.

Blowout

Splurge on an ornate mirror, the size of your bed and have it fixed to the ceiling overhead. It's daring, decadent, and deliciously dirty.

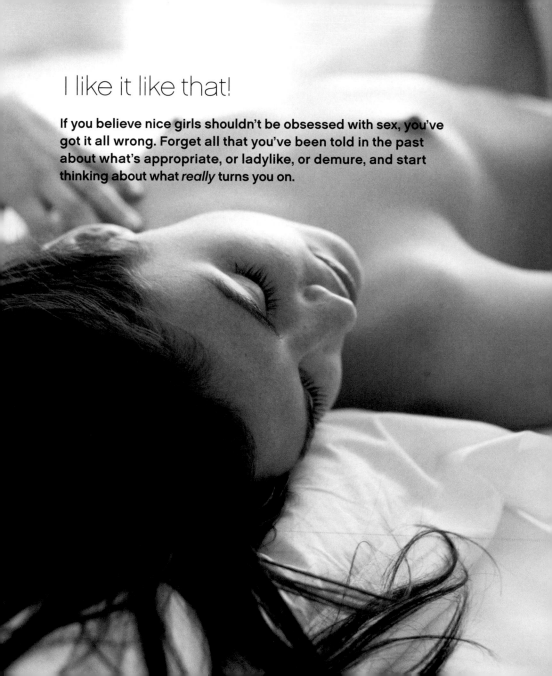

I like it like that!

If you believe nice girls shouldn't be obsessed with sex, you've got it all wrong. Forget all that you've been told in the past about what's appropriate, or ladylike, or demure, and start thinking about what *really* turns you on.

The simple fact is, if you don't know what makes you orgasm, how can you tell anyone else? Here are some things to try to help you get aroused.

Masturbating is a sure-fire way of finding out exactly what turns you on and how you most enjoy being touched. It's also great for relieving stress, making you feel good (an orgasm releases endorphins), exercising your vaginal muscles, and increasing the number of orgasms you'll actually have *avec un homme*. Here are three ways to masturbate for maximum effect:

The clitoris: rub your clitoris lightly in a circular motion, or back and forth. The tip of the clitoris is ultra-sensitive so if this is too intense, rub your pelvis up against a pillow or your mattress, or spray jets of water from the shower between your legs instead.

The G-spot: slide two fingers inside you and reach up toward your stomach. 1–2 inches up you'll find your G-spot, a spongy patch of skin about the size of a quarter. Gently but consistently rub it in a circular motion.

The A-spot: this is just above your G-spot but below your cervix. It's a smooth, extremely sensitive area about the size of a nickel that will really respond to gentle rubbing.

Fantasy island: combine this with masturbation for maximum effect. Everyone has different fantasies, from the dirtiest sex scene you ever saw in a movie to the image of that guy who you see walking his dog in the park every day, naked. If it gets you off, it's all good.

Big girl toys

Forget Barbies and stuffed animals, there are just a handful of aids you should have close to your bedside.

Vibrators
Whether it is something small and slick that can fit in your clutch bag or a massive machine with numerous heads and oscillating speeds – you're bound to find a vibrator to suit you. Hold it against your clitoris or labia for sizzling sensations.

Porn
Re-enact a blue movie together, pop a tape into your video recorder and keep up move-for-move. Playing it in mute means you can ignore the cheesy dialog and concentrate on the action instead.

Toys
Love eggs wiggle around orgasmically when you insert them inside you. Ribbed condoms give you that extra friction during sex. Lubricants make all body parts slippery and easy to insert, and clit ticklers are pretty self-explanatory. All can be found at your local sex shops – a slew of trendy sex shops have made these toys stylish, so there's no need to enter the stores incognito.

Positions
The *Karma Sutra* might be a good jumping off point, but your own imaginations should take you a whole lot further. The more flexible and gymnastic you are, the more amazing positions you'll be able to achieve and if it feels good, who cares what it looks like?

Fantasies

Spill your secrets and get him to do the same, not only will you learn a few tidbits to turn him on, you'll also improve your sexual communication and probably strengthen your relationship in the process.

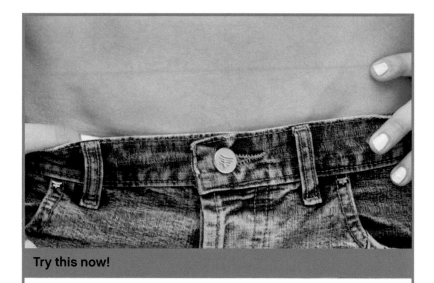

Try this now!

Head out and get yourself a "butterfly." This is a small vibrating disc that you slip over your hips and under your panties. Once in place you can stay in your bedroom if you like, but why not leave it on while you go about your daily chores. This way you can orgasm while shopping for groceries, with the sex scenes at the movies, or when things get really dull at work.

Don't ask, don't get

Now that you know what makes you quiver between the sheets (and that lesson seemed nothing like studying), you have to get that information out in the open. It can feel awkward telling a guy that his seduction skills aren't quite doing the trick but, knowing what hot, toe-curling pleasures await you, how can you lie back, smile sweetly, and let him tinker with your intimates with the tenderness of a car mechanic? The important thing is not to make his confidence (or anything else, for that matter) droop with a bitchy comment.

Instead of telling him what he's doing wrong, focus on how he can get things right. Be a goddess about it and be upfront – ask if he wants to find out exactly what drives you wild, and when he says yes (because he definitely will), use his hands and your own to squeeze and stroke you in all the right ways.

Once he's seen how easy it is to make you melt, he'll definitely use the same tricks again. If this feels way too forward, you could always try keeping quiet during the less erotic moments and making the appropriate moans and groans when he gets it right. This method may take longer, but after a while he's bound to take the hint. One last option: spill your turn-ons over email or during a late night phone call. You won't have to deal with the awkward face-to-face thing, but you'll get your feelings across with some sexual frisson thrown in too.

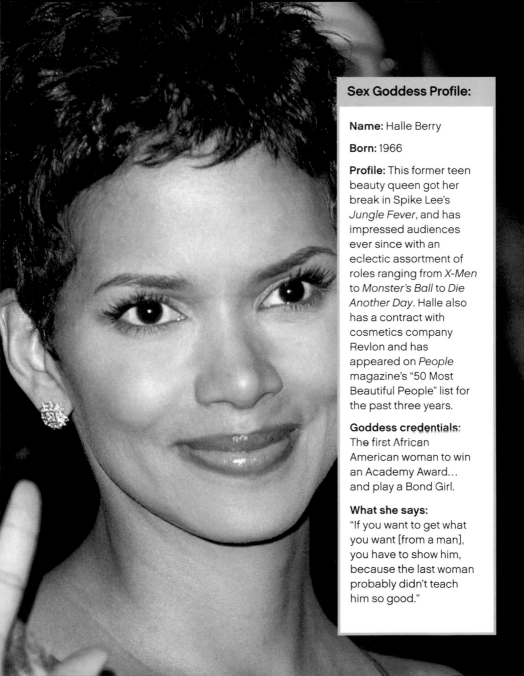

Sex Goddess Profile:

Name: Halle Berry

Born: 1966

Profile: This former teen beauty queen got her break in Spike Lee's *Jungle Fever*, and has impressed audiences ever since with an eclectic assortment of roles ranging from *X-Men* to *Monster's Ball* to *Die Another Day*. Halle also has a contract with cosmetics company Revlon and has appeared on *People* magazine's "50 Most Beautiful People" list for the past three years.

Goddess credentials: The first African American woman to win an Academy Award… and play a Bond Girl.

What she says: "If you want to get what you want [from a man], you have to show him, because the last woman probably didn't teach him so good."

How to please your man

Nothing feels better than knowing you are driving a man insane between the sheets. Being a sex vixen and being able to bring him effortlessly to the brink of orgasm is pretty damn empowering. Ask him what tips him over the edge – it's great foreplay (little gets him more aroused) – and you're bound to get turned on too simply by knowing how much carnal pleasure you're giving him. If you want to throw a little of your own creativity into the mix, here are a few surefire things he'll love in the sack (even if he doesn't quite know it yet).

Having his ears licked
This is definitely one for the early stages of foreplay, but remember that a man's ears are so much more erogenous than a woman's. It will drive him wild and leave him begging for the real action.

Having his nipples tweaked
Chances are you don't give his chest as much attention as he gives yours (but be gentle, he's just as sensitive as you), so gently rub his nipple in between your thumb and forefinger, or nibble at it, or swirl an ice cube over it.

You initiating sex
Tell him exactly where and how you want him. He may not want to have you bark orders at him every time you get dirty, but once in a while he'll get off on being overpowered by you and playing the sex slave.

You masturbating in front of him

Guys love the voyeuristic aspect of watching a woman touch herself and it's the perfect way to show him how to swirl your fingers around your clitoris and rise to an orgasm.

Shoes

No doubt you've seduced your man by parading around in a push-up bra and black lace thong, but have you ever considered ditching the threads in favor of strappy stilettos and a whole lot of skin? It works every time.

You on top

You've probably tried this facing him, but twist around so you're facing his feet. Men are also obsessed with a fine butt, so he'll really get off on staring at yours. When he comes, pull on his toes to intensify his orgasm.

Noise

You don't have to compete with Kim Catrall's howling in *Porky's*, but a few enthusiastic moans and groans will only intensify his own excitement – especially if you really mean it.

Make it public

It's wild and dangerous, but what man hasn't fantasized about a woman slipping discreetly under the table, unzipping his fly, and giving him head in the middle of a fancy restaurant? It's essential that he keeps his cool so as not to give the game away.

Suck some ice before giving him a blow job
This works even better if he doesn't know you're doing it – he'll experience an icy rush instead of the warmth of your mouth he was expecting.

A little pleasurable pain
Whips and handcuffs aren't everybody's cup of tea, but he's guaranteed to enjoy you grazing your nails lightly up his inner thighs.

Give him a full-body massage – using your entire body
He'll be driven wild by the warm scented massage oil and feeling your breasts, feet, and shoulders rubbing against every part of him.

A Brazilian wax
It may be a little painful but all that smooth skin on display never hurt the girl from Ipanema… He'll go crazy for the uninterrupted view of your vagina and he'll be even more eager to get down there and feel the softness against his cheeks.

Forget the bedroom

We can all curl up and get coital under our own sheets, but sometimes the further away you are from the bedroom, the hotter the sex becomes. If you can't imagine feeling frisky anywhere other than on a mattress, use these suggestions, tried and tested by some very creative sex goddesses, as a jumping off point...

Mallory says, "Do it in the snow: You'll need to be fast and furious to stay warm, but that's part of the fun."

Shelly suggests, "Try it in a sports stadium: When our team was on a losing streak, we'd head up to the empty cheap seats and score for ourselves."

Victoria prefers a very posh hotel, "I'd blow a fortune on the penthouse suite, but I'd make it worth the money by having sex in every conceivable corner – that includes the hot tub and on top of the mini bar!"

Kelly did it at a wedding. "Why should the bride and groom be the only ones to get intimate? When my friend Zoe got married, my then-boyfriend and I sneaked off during the reception and did some celebrating of our own."

Sarah confides, "I love doing it on the beach. Nothing makes me more horny than hot sun, crashing waves, and strutting around half naked. I've seduced a few guys in the sand."

Rosa says, "Airplane toilets are the furthest thing from sexy, but when we got upgraded to business class, which has reclining beds, extra thick blankets, and privacy screens, we thought we should take advantage of it."

Lisa likes to spice up her laundry sessions. "When we splurged on our own washing machine, I got the idea to jump on top and wait for the spin cycle before having sex. Talk about good vibrations – they totally revved up our sex. We do it every week."

Susan says, "We'd been on a road trip for a few hours when we found ourselves in the middle of nowhere, surrounded by desert and horny as hell. We pulled over for a sex break. Being in a convertible made it even more exciting."

Eva likes to sneak her boyfriend into the dressing room when she's shopping, "You've got to be quick so the sales assistant won't notice, but that makes it even more of a challenge."

Isabelle got creative in a campsite. "I got together with this guy on a hiking trip, but there wasn't exactly anywhere to get intimate, so we zipped two sleeping bags together and made a sex cocoon."

6 Sexpertise

Something extra for
sex perfection

Playing the big league

Once you've mastered the basics of sex, you can get onto the serious stuff. On the following pages, you'll find the kind of moves that set a sex goddess apart from the average girl. These are the tricks that will have guys begging not to leave your bed, they're also the secrets that all your friends wish you'd share. Whether you're practicing these with your long-term boyfriend or wowing a first-time shag, the following acts are guaranteed to help you achieve sex perfection.

Come together: if this has happened as a mere fluke in the past, you'll have marveled at how good it felt to be that connected. Now you can achieve it as often as you want. To do this you need to understand how aroused you can both become and learn how to control each level of arousal, so that you both reach the same place at the same time. It may feel weird but you should try and express how turned on you are in stages, say numbers from one to ten. Remember, it's easier for men to become aroused more quickly – a man can orgasm within three minutes of becoming excited, but a woman needs a minimum of 13, so he might be at stage eight when you're only on stage three. Show each other how much stimulation you need to climax and figure out how long it takes each of you – this will take time and many sex sessions, but by coordinating your orgasms, you'll have double the pleasure.

"Nudity is pure; if not, why were Michelangelo and Raffaello so interested in it? Nudity is something magic." Monica Bellucci

Twice as much fun: what feels better than an orgasm? How about two, or maybe even three? Although multiple orgasms are the kind of thing you read about in sex manuals and hold the same mystical, not-quite-possible allure of a unicorn, they really can be yours. There are two ways to enjoy this sought-after experience, and here they are.

Make your orgasm a whole lot longer by strengthening your pelvic floor muscles. You can do this by learning to stop yourself mid-flow while going to the bathroom. Once you've got the hang of the "clench" practice it every day on your journey to work until those inner muscles are truly buff. Now, during sex, use those same muscles to grasp his penis inside you – this will send the blood flowing into your vagina. When you feel your first orgasm coming, resist the urge to let it happen. Instead, make him stay still, so that the tingly sensations just drift away. Continue to do this a few more times when your orgasm approaches – until you can't take it anymore. Finally, let the orgasm wash over you but, when it does, continue to clench and release your pelvic muscles the way you practiced – the extra flow of blood and pelvic contractions will increase and intensify your orgasm, giving you the longest, strongest sensations ever.

Another option is to continue pumping away together after your first orgasm. It may seem strange to continue going on after you've both reached your goal and it could even feel a bit sensitive at first, but after five or ten minutes, you will orgasm again. This time it might be a shorter, sweeter release, but hey, it's still two (or three if you continue) for the price of one.

Great handiwork

See a great hand job as the promise of things to come. This is your first chance to show off your sex skills, so get it just right. Start by positioning yourself in the best place, sit astride him or get him to stand in front of you. Stroke him lightly around his inner thighs and graze his penis with your fingertips until he becomes rock hard.

Then wrap your hand around the shaft of his penis and start rubbing up and down in a regular rhythm. As you get to the head close your fist a little when you glide over it, increasing the pressure – he has more nerve endings here so a stronger touch will drive him wild.

Use both hands on his penis at one time or use one hand to massage his balls. This way you can switch from hand to hand, when one gets numb. Keep a gliding motion rather than jerking, speed up for a while then slow down again, teasing him with that orgasm. The faster you move, the quicker he'll come, so speed up your pace for the grand finale. Once he has ejaculated, remove your hands straight away as he'll become ultra-sensitive and pleasure will quickly turn to pain with one tug too many.

The perfect blow job: tease him initially by nibbling along his thighs, then circling the head of his penis and running your tongue up and down the shaft. When you finally take his penis in your mouth place one hand at the base and use it to follow your lips, rubbing up and down the shaft with your hands and mouth simultaneously to increase the friction. Use the other hand to cup and massage his balls and lightly massage his perineum (the space between his testicles and his anus). Vary your speed and intensity, graze your teeth lightly over his skin, but never bite.

Suck on his balls and tweak his nipples. If you're worried about his penis going too far back into your throat and making you gag, guide it into the side of your mouth instead and if you need to come up for breath, tickle the frenulum (the small piece of skin where the head meets the shaft) with the end of your tongue at the same time (this area is extra sensitive).

The absolute best way you can drive a man wild is to act like you love what you're doing and there's nothing you enjoy more than having his cock in your mouth (a few pleasurable moans should do the trick). Oh, and if you can bring yourself to swallow, he'll think all his birthdays and Christmasses have come at once.

Try this now!

An amazing alternative to the hand job is a boob job (and not the silicone variety). Place his penis between your breasts and squish them together so he can rub up and down between them. If your boobs are small and perky, crush them together as close as possible to create a cleavage for him to slide into. If you have voluptuous swingers, make this your specialty.

All the right moves

There's nothing wrong with a classic missionary screw once in a while, but a sex goddess (and especially one who's graduated to this chapter), likes to shake it up a bit. You don't need to be Olga Korbut to master these gymnastic moves, but the more flexible you are, the more creative your poses can be.

Woman on top: he can play with your breasts and clitoris, while you get to control the speed and intensity of the experience, feeling him deep inside you. Make things even more heated by squatting over him with your feet flat on the bed and bouncing yourself up and down. Vary the position by facing the other direction and letting him see the perfect curves of your butt – massage his balls at the same time.

Doggy style: when a guy takes you from behind, his penis pushes against your G-spot. Combine this with the fact that you can masturbate at the same time and an orgasm is almost guaranteed. Switch things up by both kneeling, or you kneel on the bed while he stands at the edge, or both stand up and let him bend you over from the waist.

Standing up: if your man has been working out, let him show off his guns, by holding you around his waist (do your bit by wrapping your legs over his hips and clenching your thighs to keep yourself up there). This position means deep penetration and amazing stimulation for your vaginal nerves. Not a muscle man? Prop yourself up against a table or a wall instead.

Spooning: for those dozy mornings when cuddling leads to sex. This position also allows you to play with your clitoris at the same time.

C.A.T.: the coital alignment technique increases your chance to orgasm together. He gets on top of you, lining his pelvis up against yours, so although the head of his penis is inside you, the shaft is pressing against your *mons pubis* (the fleshy mound covered in pubic hair). He steadies himself so his pelvis is never lower than yours and then you both rock in a synchronized motion. As you rock upward his penis slides down inside you, rubbing against your clitoris. During the downward stroke, he rocks slightly out of you again. Although this takes a little practice, there's no need to speed up the pace as the two of you should naturally reach orgasm together. Yeah baby!

Sex sagas

It can't always be blissful between the sheets, but a sex goddess knows how to deal with even the most awkward moments. Here are some solutions to those sticky situations.

STIs
Try and avoid STIs (sexually transmitted infections) in the first place by using condoms, as any rashes, skin disorders, or diseases can be painful, dangerous, and real mood killers. Avoid sex until all infections are cleared up. Don't assume just because you can't see symptoms you're good to go. Visit a gynecologist for regular check-ups.

Bondage
One girl's fantasy is another's nightmare. Being tied up and whipped could be a ton of fun, but stay in your comfort zone by choosing silk scarves over handcuffs (they're more comfortable and easier to remove), having a "safe" word that you'll use when you want the session to end, and only indulging with someone you really trust.

Boredom
Same position, same location, same time of day? Shake things up a bit and add some spontaneity to your sex. After reading this chapter you'll have a few new tips and tricks to try out.

Premature ejaculation
To increase the length of time your man can have sex, grasp the base of his penis and squeeze firmly when he's about to come. This will stop the flow of semen from his testicles and delay his orgasm.

Threesomes
Only invite a friend along if it's something you're both into (don't just do it for him). For many, three's a crowd, so establish some ground rules first, also consider how it may affect your friendships afterward.

Saying the wrong name
Oops! If you think he might not have heard, focus his attention immediately elsewhere with any mind-blowing sex act before he has time to mull it over. But if you're well and truly busted, laugh it off with as much style and panache as you can muster.

Feeling freaked out
Sex is only fun when you're both enjoying yourselves. Although you should never feel bad about what turns you on, it's different strokes for different folks. The only way to let someone know what you're cool with doing in bed and to find out what they're comfortable with, is to communicate. Never do anything that makes you feel uncomfortable, but equally don't insist anyone else does either.

Sex Goddess Profile:

Name: Brigitte Bardot

Born: 1934

Profile: The Parisian starlet modeled for French *Elle* aged 15 and, three years later, landed her first movie role – and her first husband, director Roger Vadim. Their relationship only lasted five years, but Brigitte's film career lasted over 20. At 40, she retired from movies, deciding to focus instead on her real love: animal rights.

Goddess credentials: Her bed-head bouffant and up-swept eyeliner have become the epitome of a sexy *ingénue*. Where Claudia Schiffer and Heather Graham followed, Brigitte Bardot led.

What she says: "I have always adored beautiful young men. Just because I grow older, my taste doesn't change. So if I can still have them, why not?"

Going tantric

You've probably heard many an Eastern promise about this method of sex, but have you ever tried it for yourself? To make a mystic commitment and share the tantric sex experience together, start by lying naked, facing each other and discovering your body parts without arousing each other.

Once you have done that, lie spooning each other and listening to your breath. Synchronize your breathing so that you inhale for four seconds, hold for four seconds, exhale for four seconds, and pause for four seconds. Repeat this until you are in total harmony and try to imagine your breath is entering you through your vagina and being expelled through your mouth, while he visualizes that same breath entering his mouth and leaving through his penis. This connects your chakras (the spot in between your eyebrows) and creates a circle of energy between you. After a while, turn to face each other and stare into each other's third eyes (chakras) for a few minutes.

Now sit on top of him, facing each other with your legs wrapped around his back and let him enter you. Now you do nothing, except for gaze into each other's third eyes and synchronize your breathing, as before. While in this position, flex your pelvic floor muscles (which sends blood into your vagina), he does the same, rushing blood into his penis. Marvelously, even without thrusting you'll find yourself become aroused and reaching a level of intense pleasure. Continue to breathe and relax and wait for the next, higher, level of sensation. This will go on for a while… until you both finally experience the most intense, mind-blowing orgasms ever – it's definitely worth the wait.

From pink chiffon to blue movies

If you thought we'd already covered all the kinky ways to spice up your sex life, you were wrong. These games will get you hornier than you ever thought possible...

Force fields: start naked, facing each other. Pretend there is a force field all around your bodies, which is two inches from your skin. So you can stroke each other, or pretend to massage each other's sexual organs, but you can't actually touch. The feeling of having someone almost connect with your body intensifies your cravings for their touch. Sooner or later someone will break the rules – which will make them the loser – although at this stage you will be so overcome with hard-core lust, you will both be winners.

Two blind mice: when neither of you can see each other's bodies you have to rely so much more on your other senses: touch, smell, sound, and taste. This sexual encounter will have you licking your way to each other's hot spots and relying on moans and groans to know you're getting it right.

Sets of nine: give your sex organs a massage with this Taoist technique. Let him put just the head of his penis inside you and do nine short, shallow thrusts, then one deep one where he puts the entire length inside you. Then repeat again, this time with eight shallow strokes and two deep ones at the end. Repeat once more, this time with seven shallow strokes and three deep. Continue until you end with one shallow stroke and nine deep. Bliss.

Nervous: just like the game you used to play at school, but this one's more hardcore. One person starts making some slow sexual moves, while the other assesses whether the situation is making them "nervous." This is a perfect way to explore your kinkier desires, from anal stimulation to dildos to bondage. See how he feels about your lubricated finger being pushed slowly into his butt hole. See how much you like having a strap-on eased inside you.

Blue movie: rig up the camera to a TV and play it through the screen. Do not, repeat, not, insert a tape. All those urban myths about mixing the tape up with another and playing it when your parents come to stay? They're true. Instead, think of a theme, dress up and turn your room into the scene from a sexy – or just plain blue – movie. Have the screen in plain view of the bed and play out your ultimate fantasy, whether you imagine you are staying in a faraway hotel, spending the night in a wild west saloon, or making out with a total stranger.

Try this now!

Taste Sensation: add a little flavor to your sex life by raiding the refrigerator. Drizzle honey over your nipples and let him lick it off. Squirt whipped cream into his butt crack and glide your tongue along until you've slurped it all up. Crack open a bottle of champagne and trickle it over your clitoris.

7 Conquer the World

Use your goddess charms
to help you achieve anything

How to have it all

What's the secret to having anything you want? The truth is, there isn't just one answer to this: to pursue your dreams you need different types of ammo under your belt. A crucial one is flirting. As you know, a sex goddess doesn't just flirt with men, women can also fall prey to her flattery and alluring tactics. You should use your charm and charisma to help you achieve anything you want – whether that's a job promotion, a legendary soirée, or a discount on a vacation.

"There is no point at which you can say, 'Well I'm successful now. I might as well take a nap.'" Carrie Fisher

Sweet-talking isn't the only thing you'll need to use – there's that confidence thing again – but hard work and talent are also essential. To get anywhere (or anything) in life, you have to start with determination and drive. If you *want* it enough, it will come. Then you need the will power to remain constant in your battle to get what you deserve (and you *do* deserve it). With a few clever tricks up your sleeve everything will be a cinch – it's guaranteed.

Working girl

Let's start by saying, no matter how sexy you are, and how irresistible men are to your charms, a sex goddess will never sleep her way to the top. It's just not classy – it's so much more chic to get there on your own merits. Having said that, you can use a few of your natural talents to help you climb a rung or two of the job ladder.

When it comes down to it, practically every employer on this planet is looking for someone smart, reliable, and trustworthy. What makes you stand out from the rest of the crowd is your sparkle and enthusiasm. Start as you mean to go on and show any boss-to-be that you're already ahead of the game. Say you have to fulfill some kind of brief as part of an interview. Instead of simply doing what is required to complete the task, why not think up ways of taking it further and putting a few additional ideas into your submission? It will be far more than is needed, but it will get you the job. The reason why? It's always better to do too much than too little. Prospective employers are looking for that person willing to go the extra mile, so make sure it's you.

When asking for a raise, learn to be an ace-negotiator. Explain the reasons why you deserve a raise (these should include extra responsibilities you've taken on that weren't in your job description) and find out how much money is usually paid to a person in your position.

The tough news is, most people are ready for a promotion long before the bigwigs see fit to give it to them. Before you ask for one, make sure you've done everything you can do to earn a new title. This should include: asking for more responsibilities, staying late to get extra work done (and to show you're committed) and finding out what the new position entails so you're prepared for what you'll be taking on.

On the subject of relationships at work, having frissons with every man in your office is definitely not advised. Try to curb some of your flirtier techniques (no pressing him up against the water cooler) and simply see men as colleagues. If this is absolutely impossible and you just have to get intimate with one of your coworkers, keep your personal and professional lives separate. Save the pet names, making out, and arguments for home.

There will always come a time when you have to move on. No job is going to be stimulating all of the time, but if you've got to the stage where you can do yours with your eyes closed, ask for more work or different challenges. As soon as you feel you've mastered what you're doing, hunt for something new – even if this means a brand new job. Treading water is eventually going to leave you uninspired and unfulfilled.

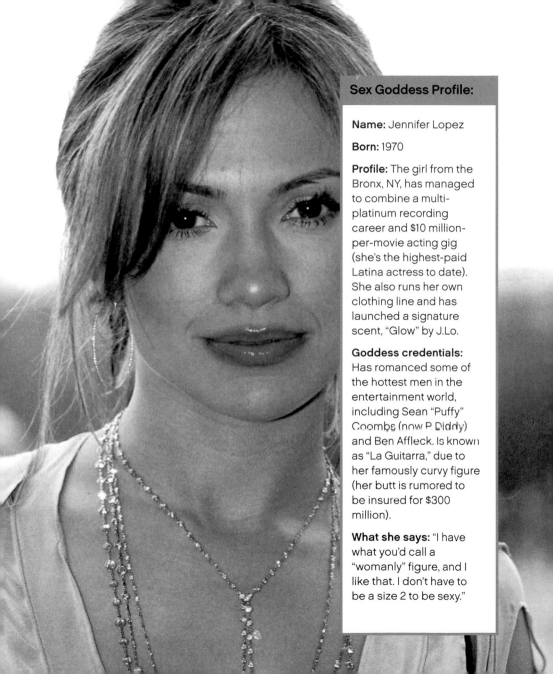

Sex Goddess Profile:

Name: Jennifer Lopez

Born: 1970

Profile: The girl from the Bronx, NY, has managed to combine a multi-platinum recording career and $10 million-per-movie acting gig (she's the highest-paid Latina actress to date). She also runs her own clothing line and has launched a signature scent, "Glow" by J.Lo.

Goddess credentials: Has romanced some of the hottest men in the entertainment world, including Sean "Puffy" Coombs (now P. Diddy) and Ben Affleck. Is known as "La Guitarra," due to her famously curvy figure (her butt is rumored to be insured for $300 million).

What she says: "I have what you'd call a "womanly" figure, and I like that. I don't have to be a size 2 to be sexy."

The green-eyed monster

Jealousy is one of the worst feelings ever. Whether you resent another woman, or she's envious of you, it's a no-win situation. So let's start with quashing your own green-eyed monster. Jealousy stems from insecurity and low self-esteem. Hopefully, most of the time, you're confident and content, but on those occasions you feel the envy rising, check yourself.

What is making you feel this way? Is it something you too can achieve or are you craving something totally out of your reach? It is true that a little competitive rivalry compels you to do better, work harder, reach further, but only if you can keep a sense of proportion about it. Jealousy is ugly, but drive and desire are things worth finding within the emotion. If your feelings are making you miserable, the best thing to do is face them head on. Tell the person of whom you are envious how you feel and why – chances are there are aspects of your life/character/body that she's equally impressed by – things you might have forgotten you even had going for you. Getting your feelings out in the open will hopefully diminish them or at least boost your own self-esteem. If you can't face your foe, reveal that jade-eyed monster to your close friends instead, for the morale boost you need.

When someone is being bitchy and catty toward you – and you have a pretty good idea it stems from jealousy – take the higher ground. It is far more graceful to ignore the snide comments and instead win her over with your warmth and charm. Don't bite back, but go to the other extreme and tell her what you admire about her. Your flattery should make her feel more self-assured and crush her caustic feelings.

Up, up, and away…

It is pretty obvious that a sex goddess likes to travel, and it should not be underestimated just how important it is for you to spread your wings. As a glorious, open-minded woman you need to fill your head with new places, exciting experiences, and to become inspired by goddesses the world over. The more money you can put aside, the better.

Remember to do your homework before you set your manicured foot onto foreign soils, however. This means buying a good travel guide and retiring for a long soak in the bath. Also, attempt to learn the lingo. A phrase book should suffice for the essentials ("How much is it?" "Where is the bathroom?") before you go.

Once you have secured an upgrade on your flight, there are a few other tricks for making the journey a whole lot more comfortable, (a pair of velour sweatpants packed in your hand luggage, for example.) Alcohol may be free but will leave you dehydrated and groggy, so stick to water and bring a bag of trail mix to nibble on instead of the bland airplane fare. As soon as you have charmed the check-in staff, wipe off your make-up and replace with a layer of thick moisturizer (to combat the hard-core air conditioning) and avoid DVT (deep vein thrombosis) by doing a few yoga stretches in the aisle whenever you get the chance.

When in Rome… or Barcelona, or Paris, or Marrakech, take lifestyle props from the locals. The only way to immerse yourself in their culture is to leave your normal routine at home. So sample the different dishes, steer clear of tourist traps, and befriend a few locals to take you sightseeing.

Savvy goddess

You don't need to be rolling in cash to live like you're mega-rich. Sex goddesses often wow others with their thrifty methods of getting what they want. Here are some tips to help you on your way to the good life. Get more bang for your buck…

… **on vacation:** when booking your jaunt to sunnier climes, first find your dream location, then hunt for the cheapest deal. The prices quoted in holiday brochures are always inflated so refuse to pay that amount. Speak to travel agents and ask what deal they can get for you, or search online for special offers. For last minute trips you can barter even more and check out the websites dedicated to securing you a flight and hotel for a shockingly rock-bottom price.

… on airplanes: dressing nicely used to be the best way to get an upgrade, now being a member of the airline's frequent-flyer program is a surer bet that you'll be looked at favorably (signing up is free). Smart threads still cut it – as does a polite request (act entitled and you won't stand a chance). If an upgrade is out of the question, early birds can ask to sit by an exit, which means a ton more legroom (it also helps if you have a 6' 4" boyfriend!).

… in restaurants: book well in advance to ensure you'll snag a reservation. Scope out the joint beforehand so you can request a particular table. If the prices are just too high for your budget, ask if they have a prix fixe menu, or order two appetizers (usually half the price of an entrée) and insist you have a small appetite. Prices are often reduced at lunchtime too.

… in shops: check if your favorite store has a mailing list – most do and once you're on it, you'll be kept up to date with sales and offered discounts. Make friends with a sales assistant, always get her to serve you, and build a rapport. She'll probably waiver a no-hold policy for you and may even call when new items come in. (Buddy up with the store's manager and it's your lucky day.)

… in beauty stores: swanky beauty counters don't appreciate scroungers, so don't march up to the counter and expect them to dole out free samples. On the other hand, you could splash out on a soap (usually one of the cheapest products available), enquire about other items, and end up going home with a bag of samples. Ask if they have products in travel-size – these are often given away as freebies and you'll be surprised how long a mini pot of eye cream can actually last.

Be smart, be sassy, be safe

Here's how...

* Always save enough cash for the entire cab fare home – including the tip.

* Whenever going somewhere new, buy a map and get as familiar with your surroundings as possible.

* Don't jog with a personal CD player on, as it stops you being alert and aware of what's going on around you.

* Keep your cell phone fully charged – you never know when you may need it.

* Never collect your car from a multi-storey car park alone – cough up the extra for a valet.

* Learn where your fuse box is in your apartment before a blackout.

* Let at least one person know where you are at all times.

* Travel light – if you can fit your wheeled luggage case into an overhead compartment you'll never have to stand in line at lost and found again.

* Keep precious jewelry somewhere random, like in an egg carton in the fridge or stuffed in an old sock – where no burglar would ever think to look.

* Never go to sleep with your lavender-scented aromatherapy candle still burning.

* Learn how to change a tire – you never know when it might come in useful.

* Don't go home with a total stranger – no matter how hot he is.

* Take self-defense classes. If you never end up using them, even better.

* When traveling abroad always carry around the details of the place where you're staying and learn how to ask, "*donde esta?*" in the appropriate language.

* Carry an alarm – the noise will hopefully scare away any potential attacker and alert everyone else's attention.

8 When the Going gets Tough

How a sex goddess
survives *any* situation

When life ain't so smooth

Sometimes life can be pretty crappy – just when everything else in your world falls into place, there's one thing that screws it up. It could be a harrowing break-up with the guy you thought was your soul mate, getting laid off from a great job, having an infuriating bust-up with your parents, or realizing you are so far into the red that you can't remember a time when you were debt-free. Sadly a sex goddess isn't immune to life's foul-ups, but she does know how to handle them better than most.

There are those tiny things that can really bug you – a snippy argument with a close friend, a tear in your favorite pants, gaining a few pounds. Taken one at a time, these are the kinds of things you can shrug off, but a day of them (especially a pre-menstrual day) can seem like the end of the world. Face these problems head on – after you've had a chance to seethe and curse (under your breath – there's nothing tackier than a lady hollering swear words in the street), suck it up and rectify these minor impositions as quickly as you can.

Then there's the big sh*t. Losing your job, accruing horrifying debt, accidentally becoming pregnant, a nasty end to a good friendship, divorce, death. This is the stuff that is going to take a lot more time – emotionally and literally – to come to terms with.

In any kind of hardship, it's important that you acknowledge your lows and recognize that the only way is up and that you intend to get there with as much dignity and grace as possible. There's no such thing as "wallowing" in your misery – you should do your crying in private, or at least in the arms of your closest friend or partner. Remember, whatever happens, when the going gets tough a sex goddess just gets tougher.

"Just don't give up trying to do what you really want to do. Where there is love and inspiration, I don't think you can go wrong." Ella Fitzgerald

Stay positive: don't crawl into a hole and hope it will all go away – rise to the occasion. You must be determined to overcome it, trying to find a way to make things better. If you don't find it as easy to get peppy again, surround yourself with practical, positive friends who will happily help you find that silver lining and focus on the problem solving.

Rising to the challenge

Being brave and dealing with tough situations is a sure-fire way to boost your confidence. Different things freak out different people — a party where you don't know anyone, a blind date, skydiving — whatever makes your knees knock is worth trying once. Again, don't expect this is to be a walk in the park: you will feel scared, but that's the point.

The exhilaration you'll experience once you've completed your task will make it all worthwhile. Don't stop there, though. Keep pushing yourself, watch your confidence grow, and take pleasure in kicking your fear in the butt.

Every time you do something that makes you feel good — write it down. If you can't think of anything more tedious than writing a journal, keep a mini-notebook in your bag instead and just jot down a few words each time. It can be anything: you called your grandmother, you avoided the 3 pm doughnut craving, you bought a cup of coffee for a homeless person. When you're feeling blue, flick through your list and remind yourself of the things you feel good about.

This works the other way around too. At your lowest moments, make a note of what's getting you down. When you're feeling more rational, read through your entries and look for a pattern. If you discover you're generally unhappy with one area of your life or at certain times in your life (PMS anyone?) you can work with the information and try to do something about it.

Love and war

Even the best of relationships hit stony ground once in a while. There are naturally going to be times when you don't see eye to eye, or your beau does something to really enrage you. Depending on how long you've been together and how much you like the guy, you have two choices:

* Dump him.
* Work through it.

If you choose the latter, you'll need to bear some things in mind. The first is communication, which is essential. Refusing to call him until he apologizes may work, but could also leave you single again. Calmly discussing how you both feel is more likely to help you reach a solution. Remember, men are generally useless at discussing their feelings so this may not be a cinch, but you should get there in the end. Compromise is important, but so is staying true to your beliefs; evaluate every issue that comes between you and try to find a resolution that suits you both. Some things will never change and these will be the things you either learn to live with or that eventually get the better of you.

Once you have your man hooked, you want him to stay that way. Keeping the relationship hot means not getting stuck in a rut or letting things slide. Remember what attracted you to each other in the first place – your adventurous spirit, your sex appeal, your attitude and ideas. Maintain these elements of your character and five years together will still seem like five days. Be spontaneous – book random weekends away or crazy things to do together (ever learnt to ride a trapeze?). Spend a day naked – order sushi and let him eat it off your belly. Relive the flirting techniques that captured him in the first place. Make a Saturday night date together and each arrange part of the night – one choosing a restaurant, the other making after-dinner plans.

Budget

Send him a lacy thong, in a box wrapped in brown paper. Attach a parcel tag stating the time and location that you intend to wear it. He'll set his alarm the moment he receives it.

Blowout

Book a weekend in Hawaii. Slip into a grass skirt, order your favorite cocktail and watch the sun set before embarking on a night of unbridled Polynesian passion.

Sex Goddess Profile:

Name: Jackie Onassis

Born: 1929

Profile: "Debutante of the Year" for 1947–1948, Jacqueline Lee Bouvier met Senator Kennedy while working at a local newspaper. They married in 1953 and Jackie took her role as First Lady seriously, devoting time and study to make the White House a museum of American history.

Goddess credentials: Despite outliving two husbands, Jackie never gave up her independent spirit. In later years she moved to New York City and worked as an editor for Doubleday.

What she says: "The good, the bad, hardship, joy, tragedy, love, and happiness are all interwoven into one indescribable whole that one calls life. You cannot separate the good from the bad, and perhaps there is no need to do so."

Ciao baby

"I say goodbye to love." "Every time we say goodbye, I cry a little." "Bye, bye love." It's a lot easier to sing about splitting up with a guy than actually to do it. But sometimes you have to bite the bullet. A sex goddess knows she's too good to date a scumbag, and even if he hasn't actually wronged you, there are still times when "so long" are the only words you should utter. Here are a few of them.

When he's two-timing you: a goddess never shares her men, so if he's into playing the field it's time to relegate him to the bench.

When he disses you: you're pretty amazing and if he doesn't get that, he's the one with the problem. Anyone who regularly criticizes your body, clothes, personality, or lifestyle isn't worth having around.

When he doesn't live up to his promises: if he talks the talk, he'd better walk the walk. Everyone loves weekends away, love gifts, and regular phone calls, but if all you're actually receiving is the promise of these things, don't hold your breath any longer.

When he's going nowhere: struggling artists – gorgeous, wannabe rock stars – adorable. But at what point are you going to stop paying the check and acting like his personal assistant? Vibrant, determined women deserve men with the same attitude, so don't waste your time with a dead-end guy.

When sport is more important that you are: so, he likes watching the game – what's the problem? The problem is if he chooses an evening in front of the box instead of a hot night out with you – every time. Buy him a six-pack and say "Ciao baby".

Unlucky in love

If relationships were easy, country singers would have nothing to write about and great aunts wouldn't be able to patronizingly mutter, "more fish in the sea" or "it's better to have loved and lost…" Here are a few of the crappy things you could have to face on the way to finding your perfect (or almost perfect) guy.

Sayonara sweetie: being dumped sucks, but it's okay, it's good to wallow in your depression for a few days. Loll around in your flannel PJs, play the weepiest love ballads, eat Frosties straight from the box – mourn the end of the relationship. When you've had enough of feeling sad, rally your friends around you and go out more, take up new pursuits, be open to meeting people. Accept that even if it's tough at first you will move on and the most valuable things you've taken from the relationship are experience and enlightenment. You're one step closer to finding someone worthy of you.

The wrong guy: why do some of us just seem to attract the bad guys? He seemed so great in the beginning… or maybe he didn't and that's subconsciously what attracted you to him. Decide if the reason you pick these kind of men to date is because you know ultimately they are wrong for you and you won't have to think about anything long-term. If you're positive you're not a commitment-phobe, the next step is to date guys who aren't your type. Of course, you've got to find him the teeniest bit attractive, but if creative types attract you, then end up being too self absorbed, try dating a banker. Or if you're lured by the spunky nature of a jock, but eventually find him too laddish, an artsy guy could have the sensitivity you've been missing.

Wanting what you can't have: nothing is more infuriating than meeting the man of your dreams… and finding out he's already taken. Or that he doesn't feel the same way about you. The truth is, this is a no-win situation, whichever way you look at it. A sex goddess never steals another woman's man (too tacky for words) and do you really want to be with a guy who doesn't totally adore you back? Sure, he could grow to love you, but let him do that in his own time, while you continue to play the field.

Cheating heart: having your heart broken is hard enough, but when it's because he's slept with someone else the pain is almost intolerable. Most people really can't get past this. Once your trust has been abused it can be beyond difficult to return to normality again. So you have two choices: dump him or try to move past it together. You probably can't forgive him, and he shouldn't expect you to. Try and communicate how you feel and don't let him put any blame on you – this was all him.

Sex goddess pick-me-ups

Whatever it is that has ruined your day, you cannot let it get you down forever. Here are ten ways to raise your spirits (splash out on the blowout suggestions, or bash your blues bargain-basement-style with the budget suggestions).

Budget

* Dance in the rain. Leave your umbrella at home, twirl through the puddles and let yourself get totally soaked – then warm up again in a long, soothing bath.

* Bake a cake from scratch – there's something cathartic about baking (and not from a mix), plus your kitchen will smell divine. Once you're done, treat yourself to a huge guilt-free slice.

* Go to bed early. Take a big glass of wine, or a mug of hot chocolate and a few un-opened magazines. Spend the next few hours flicking and sipping.

* Buy your favorite movie on video (the funnier the better) when you're feeling blue, put it on and get lost in that world for a while.

* Find some water – the sea, a lake, a swimming pool, even a puddle. Sit and reflect or dive right in (not the puddle). Water draws out the negative ions from your body, so you're left with only positives.

Blowout

* Rent a convertible for a day. Put the top down, pump up the music and feel the wind whistle through your hair.

* Plan a weekend away with your best friends. Take the train, find a family-run B&B, and stay up all night talking.

* Take a lunch hour, when you'd normally stay tied to your desk. Go to a fancy restaurant and order a lovely meal for one, take a newspaper. Or sit in the park for an hour with a good book. Or splurge on a pair of party shoes that you just can't resist.

* Buy little gifts for each of your friends. Focusing the attention on them will take your mind off your woes and making others happy in turn brightens your day.

* Get a lavish beauty treatment like an aromatherapy wrap or a massage. Even if you can't see the effects of these treatments, you'll certainly feel them. Bliss!

9 Celebrating your Status

Live like a goddess for
the rest of your days

Congratulations!!

You are a fully-fledged sex goddess – a Jennifer Lopez, a Sophia Loren, a Marilyn Monroe, a Halle Berry. You are one of those women who men gaze at greedily and who women admire wistfully. You're a female who knows what she wants and understands what makes her happy.

You actively work to keep your body, strong, fit, and healthy and you accept (and even sometimes adore) your reflection (even in a bikini!). Your style is phenomenal, because you have the daring and dash to wear exactly what suits you (to hell with high fashion) and you no longer flinch at a price tag in triple-figures (if it's really worth it, you'll just save up).

Guys are entranced by your charms and even if you haven't yet found the one who knocks your socks off, you certainly have a line of them willing to try. And for the lucky few who make it to the sack with you (because why just limit it to one?), your new, improved sex skills will mean earth-shattering orgasms for the both of you.

Your career path is lined with roses now that you know how to get that promotion and negotiate the salary that is yours for the taking. You also have the sass and street smarts to make the other areas of your existence run smoothly – including your relationships, home, and social life. And hey, if the sh*t hits the fan every once in a while – you even know how to handle that with skill and grace. You're a hell of a lady – you should be proud.

Now let's keep it that way…

The future's bright

Being a sex goddess is a lifetime commitment. It doesn't stop once you've found the man, or the job, of your dreams. The attitude that you now possess – that charisma and confidence – will remain with you from this day forth. No matter what you choose to do with your life, you will approach every step of it a sex goddess.

If you marry, celebrate your wedding as only a goddess would see fit – with a huge party. Invite all the important people in your life (this excludes great aunts you've never met) and party all night long. Marry for love and no other reason. Communicate. Be friends as well as lovers. Laugh. Never lose the sparkle. Don't stop enjoying the sex. Never forget why you chose him. Celebrate your anniversaries with more wild parties. Grow old together but never grow tired.

Sex goddesses make amazing mothers. They love their bodies already and even more so when they experience the miracle of a baby growing inside. They actually feel sexier when pregnant – who doesn't love glossy hair and amazingly glowy skin? They'll be wearing satin slip dresses and stilettos à la Sarah Jessica Parker, or skin-tight tank tops to show off the extra curves, they'll ignore big maternity panties in favor of Elle McPherson's skimpy *Intimates Maternelle* range and they'll still be having amazing sex – they'll just have to limit their positions for a while!

Kids of sex goddesses can't decide whether to be hopelessly proud of their moms (they're the coolest women in the playground) or horribly embarrassed (because they're the ones wolf whistling

during school sports events). Show your babies how to be confident and carefree. Let your daughter be a fashionista from an early age – even if she chooses to wear her fairy dress with wellies. Teach your son how to cook, so another woman doesn't have to down the line. Raise mini gods and goddesses.

When the kids fly the coop you get to celebrate your status even more. Do the housework naked, make love on the dining room table again, spend your entire day in bed sipping champagne and reading crappy novels. Blow your cash wildly and pamper yourself the way you did before you were packing school lunches and saving up for college educations. See your kid's departure, not as being fired from motherhood, but as a chance to start making yourself number one again, and an opportunity to marvel at their achievements while not cramping their style.

Man overboard? Divorce or separation can either be relieving or petrifying. But a goddess is not afraid to face the world alone. Look at this as a chance to start afresh – it's time to redefine your taste and let the new you emerge (no need to compromise your style anymore). Times may have changed, but inside you're still as gorgeous as you always were. When you decide to start dating again, focus on a man with intellectual beauty rather than a great hair style or biceps – now's your chance to connect on a higher level. Likewise, leave the miniskirts and heavy eyeliner to the twenty-somethings. This time around lure men with your grace and poise.

Sex Goddess Profile:

Name: Jennifer Aniston

Born: 1969

Profile: The Greek-American lost 30 pounds from her fabulous frame before she won her role as Rachel Green on the hit TV comedy *Friends*. But more great things followed, including marriage to possibly the world's most gorgeous man, Brad Pitt.

Goddess credentials: She wears designer dresses like a second skin, but admits she feels just as comfortable (and certainly looks just as hot) in casual duds. She eschews a celebrity lifestyle in favor of take-out and a movie with Brad – then again, who wouldn't?

What she says: "If someone loves you more if you're thinner, get rid of them."

Grow as a goddess

No matter how kick-ass you are already, there's always room to grow. Don't look at this as trying to mend bad ways, but view it as improving on perfection! Fed up of your elders telling you you've got the world at your feet? Well they're right – you've got the chance to do and be whatever you want. So start making some choices.

Be a sucker for making New Year's resolutions. Your friends may groan when you cajole them into writing a list of goals each January, but show them it's a chance to sit down and think about where you want to be a year from now. Writing your aims on paper and sharing them with everyone else will only make you more determined to succeed. Find a formula that works for you, and make all your goals realistic and specific. Aims that are totally unachievable or too random to actually quantify are a recipe for disaster. Try and set yourself challenges like getting a two thousand dollar pay rise or visiting the gym three times a week instead of two.

The other important thing, is not to make all your goals boring or "self-improving." Try to achieve a balance between fun stuff you really want to do but never get around to (like seeing more plays and ballets or spending more weekends out of the city) and things you'd like to strive for (like buying fewer clothes, but spending more money on the things you do get – a perfect excuse to blow cash on designer bags and shoes!). Combine these more whimsical (but nevertheless important) goals with your career aims and suddenly the list of resolutions doesn't appear so agonizing.

" I'm not interested in age. People who tell me their age are silly. You're as old as you feel." Elizabeth Arden

Honor Blackman, Lauren Hutton, Ellen Burstyn, Lauren Bacall. They're all stunning older women who still drive men wild. What's their secret? Their attitudes are young – they're open to change and take on new challenges with vigor and enthusiasm. They've also aged gracefully – avoiding teenage fashions and knowing exactly what suits them. Follow their lead and your teenage grandsons will worship you… and their friends will harbor secret crushes on you. Remain a sex goddess and you'll never stop attracting the boys!

Sex forever

The biggest trap long-term couples fall into is forgetting how much fun sex can be. It's so easy to forgo the foreplay and just resort to having a "quickie" once or twice a week – which can be unfulfilling and orgasm-free. Moving in together means sex on tap (woo-hoo!), but often results in taking it for granted and losing the enticing allure of seeing each other naked (bah!) Don't let this happen to you.

Stop sex from becoming routine by refusing to do it at the same time in the same place. If you usually have sex at night, just before you go to bed, set your alarm for 30 minutes earlier than normal in the morning and give him the sexiest wake-up call he could ask for. If you only get around to it at weekends, get some midweek action by ambushing him the moment you get in from work. Have some 6 pm sex that can linger on all night.

Shake things up by taking them outside the bedroom or spice it up with toys, explicit flicks, and by telling each other dirty tales. Remember it's all about the foreplay (without this, it's almost impossible for us girls to get aroused). Get turned on again by having foreplay-only nights. This is when he can only stroke, lick, and scratch, but he can't actually enter you. Do the same for him and see how randy you can make each other. Can't hold back? Fine, have the sex too – but if you start out this way, at least you'll both be aroused enough to enjoy it (and come at the end of it).

Don't fall into a foreplay routine either, if you can sense where he'll touch you next, before he's even got there, you need to shake things up. Nominate three of your body parts as "hot spots" (include your breasts and vagina as these are probably areas he instantly heads to during foreplay) and say that he must spend time on five other body parts first. Hopefully he'll discover some random new erogenous zones, like the backs of your knees, the soles of your feet, and your armpits. You could also try blind-folding him so he has to feel his way to your warmest bits, which should put a stop to his methodical amour.

You got to give a little...

When you're as blessed as most goddesses are, there is only one choice – to give a little something in return. The funny thing about charity work is, no matter how much you try to be altruistic, you can't help but get a kick out of making other people's lives a bit better. Bizarrely, there's nothing more hip right now than a charity event – it's a chance to throw on a party dress, socialize with your friends, see and be seen, and it's all for a good cause. Although there's nothing wrong with splashing out on a hot ticket to a benefit, a fancy soirée isn't the only way to show support.

Time is a more precious commodity than money, so if you can't spare the pennies why not donate a few hours instead. Find something that will make use of your talents – if you are great with kids, try getting involved with Save the Children, where you can give up weekends to help run fund-raising events. Or, on a global scale, consider becoming an active member of an organization like UNICEF. There are countless ways you can help, both in your own country and internationally, in bringing awareness of children's suffering to others. At the very least you can make a donation, buy gifts and cards, or read correspondence from children all over the world.

Pick a cause that appeals to you and use your charm, energy, and imagination to make a difference.

While you're saving the world superheroine-style, don't forget the environment. And here's how:

* Recycle wherever possible (look for products that contain the greatest post-consumer recycled content).

* Buy organic – which not only tastes better and is better for your body but, because it's pesticide-free, is better for the environment too.

* Walk instead of taking the car (to reduce the amount of carbon dioxide in the atmosphere).

* Switch your light bulbs for energy efficient fluorescent ones; only buy appliances with the EPA Energy Star label (these use 20 to 40 percent less energy than standard models).

* Invest your money in companies that are dedicated to protecting the environment.

* Give a monthly donation to Greenpeace.

Spread the love

Life's pretty great when you're a goddess. Sure, there will be ups and downs along the way, but there are also so many marvelous things ahead. Now you've come to the end of the book, let's hope you're feeling excited, ambitious, and ready to ditch this guide and embark on your new, sizzling, sensational life. But even if you're merely skimming through these last few pages, there is one more request to be made of you: spread the love.

We're the lucky ones, the women who have chased away our body demons and found our signature style. We're the ones who know how to look after ourselves and be in charge of our own careers. We're those sultry sisters who can pretty much get any guy we want simply by turning on the charm (and once those fellas have had a taste of us – they're not going anywhere). But there are women out there who aren't so lucky. They're stuck in a world of unshapely sweatpants and humiliating ordeals. As you probably remember (flick back to chapter two if you're experiencing a memory blip), the first step on the path to sex goddess is building your self-esteem. But one of the coolest things about sharing the wealth is helping other women on their way.

Next time you see a woman in the evilly-lit department-store fitting rooms, trying on a dress that looks good (despite the dodgy overhead fluros) – tell her. When a fellow *femme* gets promoted at work, shoot her an email to send your congrats.

See a sweaty broad giving it her all on an elliptical machine at the gym? High-five her in the locker room afterward. These tiny gestures may seem irrelevant, but they're like a sprinkling of confidence dust and could be the first steps to creating another sex goddess.

Try this now!

Now you're finished with this book, keep it somewhere safe, for those moments you need to be reassured of your goddess status. When you are feeling generous, think of a friend who you know is a sex goddess in-the-making, buy a copy of the book for her, and tie a pink satin ribbon around it before you pass it on.

This edition first published by
Barnes & Noble, Inc., by arrangement
with Elwin Street Limited.

M 10 9 8 7 6 5 4 3 2 1

ISBN 0-7607-4711-3

Conceived and produced by
Elwin Street Limited
35 Charlotte Road
London EC2A 3PD
www.elwinstreet.com

Designer: Esther Kirkpatrick

Picture Credits
Getty – page 4, 17, 18, 32, 36, 39, 43, 46, 48,
50, 52, 54, 57, 59, 61, 62, 66, 68, 75, 76, 79, 85,
86, 88, 95, 119, 125, 128, 132, 138, 143
Rex – 13, 22, 27, 41, 65, 81, 96, 107, 134
Corbis – 6, 8, 28, 70, 110, 122
Photonica – 114, 126
Iconica – 102, 112, 137

Printed in Singapore

BARNES
&NOBLE
BOOKS